Favorite Tasty and Simple Menu Ideas

A Cookbook of 100+ Light Recipes for All Occasions

Alexandra Nichols

Copyright © 2020 by Alexandra Nichols

All rights reserved. No part of this publication may be reproduced, distributed, or transmitted in any form or by any means, including photocopying, recording, or other electronic or mechanical methods, without the prior written permission of the publisher, except in the case of brief quotations embodied in critical reviews and certain other noncommercial uses permitted by copyright law.

Thank you for supporting the rights of the author and publisher.

Contents

INTRODUCTION 8
Chapter 1 «MEAL PLANS» 11
   FACTORS AFFECTING MEAL PLANS 12
   MEAL PLAN TIPS 13
   THE IMPORTANCE OF MEAL PLANS: THREE REASONS 13
   THINGS TO REMEMBER ABOUT MEAL PLANNING 17
Chapter 2 «BREAKFAST RECIPES» 18
   THE BENEFITS OF BREAKFAST 18
   THE IMPORTANCE OF BREAKFAST FOR CHILDREN 19
   A HEALTHY BREAKFAST 20
   IDEAS FOR MAKING HEALTHY BREAKFASTS 21
   BREAKFAST FOR THE LAZY 23
   BUCKWHEAT BREAKFAST 25
   FRENCH BREAKFAST 28
   LOW-CALORIE BREAKFAST 30
   FRENCH CROUTONS FOR BREAKFAST 32
   CURD BUNS FOR BREAKFAST 34
   PEASANT BREAKFAST 36
   POTATO AND HAM SLICES FOR BREAKFAST 38
   LUSH PANCAKES FOR BREAKFAST 40
   STRAWBERRY BREAKFAST 42
   EGG SALSA SANDWICHE 44
   HEALTHY BREAKFAST 46
   POTATO PANKECES 47

- CURD AND HONEY OR BREAKFAST FOR YOUR SELF 49
- FRIED EGG WITH ZUCCHINI FOR BREAKFAST 51
- SCRAMBLED EGGS FOR BREAKFAST 53
- CHEESECAKES FOR BREAKFAST 55
- CURD BREAKFAST WITH MANGO AND ORANGE 57
- TAMAGOYAKI FOR BREAKFAST 59
- FRUIT BREAKFAST WITH NUTS 61
- APPLE AND OAT SMOOTHIE FOR BREAKFAST 63
- KHACHAPURI FOR BREAKFAST 65
- CROUTONS WITH TOMATOES AND CHEESE FOR BREAKFAST 67
- RAISIN BUNS FOR BREAKFAST 69
- BREAKFAST CAKE WITH EGGS AND SAUSAGE 71

CHAPTER 3 «DESSERT RECIPES» 73
- HEALTHY DESSERTS 73
- WAYS TO MAKE DESSERT HEALTHY 74
- PINEAPPLE WITH LIME AND HONEY 75
- NO-BAKE CURD DESSERT 76
- NO-BAKE SWEDISH DESSERT (CHOKLADBOLLAR) .. 78
- NO-BAKE BERRY FRUIT DESSERT 80
- NO-BAKE ALMOND APRICOT DESSERT 82
- THIN PANCAKES IN MILK 84
- CLASSIC CHARLOTTE 86
- BLUEBERRY AND NUTMEG MUFFINS 88
- CARROT CUPCAKES WITH GINGER AND CINNAMON 91
- OATMEAL RAISIN COOKIES WITH SESAME SEEDS 93

COTTAGE CHEESE DONUTS IN ICING SUGAR 95
TRADITIONAL NAPOLEON CAKE 97
GINGER COOKIES WITH VANILLA SUGAR 100
TSVETAEVA APPLE PIE 102
"PIGEON'S MILK" CAKE 104
QUICHE LORRAINE WITH SPINACH 107
KUTABY WITH HERBS 110
SACHER TORTE 112
FAST TIRAMISU WITH RASPBERRIES AND MINT 115
CHOCOLATE FONDANT WITH ICE CREAM 117
VANILLA CREME BRULEE 120
MERINGUE WITH CARDAMOM 123
PLUM CRUMBLE 125
BASBOUSA 127
STRAWBERRY PIE WITH CRÈME PATISSIER 129
PUMPKIN PIE 132

CHAPTER 4 «LUNCH RECIPES» 134
The Importance of a Healthy Lunch 134
Nutritious lunch 136
CREAMY KOHLRABI SPIRALS WITH CHICKEN BREAST 137
ZUCCHINI MEATBALLS WITH MOZZARELLA 140
PASTA WITH CHARD AND BACON 143
POTATO PANCAKES FILLED WITH CHEESE 145
ASIAN CHICKEN WINGS WITH STRAWBERRY AND MELON SALAD 148
TATAR AZU 151
RATATOUILLE 153

IDAHO POTATOES 155
GRATIN DAUPHINOIS 157
CARROT CUTLETS 159
COD WITH TOMATOES 161
SHRIMP AND CHICKEN PAELLA 163
HAKE IN GREEN GARLIC SAUCE 166
BURGUNDY BEEF 168
CHICKEN PICASSO 171
BEEF STROGANOFF 174
KHINKALI 176
CHICKEN LIVERS IN SOUR CREAM 180
LAZY CABBAGE ROLLS WITH CHICKEN 182
CHICKEN KIEV CUTLETS 185
MASHED POTATOES 188
MINT-CRUSTED LAMB LEG 191
BEEF DUMPLINGS 193
BEEF WITH OYSTER SAUCE 195
CHICKEN WITH YOGURT, SESAME SEEDS, LEMON, AND GARLIC SAUCE 197
BAKED CHICKEN WITH VEGETABLES 199
ROSEMARY CHICKEN 202

CHAPTER 5 «DINNER RECIPES» 204
Dinner before bed 204
Early dinner 205
CROWN ROAST OF PORK WITH MUSHROOM DRESSING 206
BACON-WRAPPED PESTO PORK TENDERLOIN 208
PRIME RIB WITH FRESH HERB SAUCE 210

DUCK BREASTS WITH APRICOT CHUTNEY 213
PORK TENDERLOIN WITH THREE-BERRY SALSA 216
ITALIAN ROULADE 218
WHOLE BALSAMIC ROAST CHICKEN 221
SLOW-SIMMERED BEEF STEW 223
PINEAPPLE HAM WITH BROWN SUGAR 225
DAD'S FAMOUS STUFFIES 227
ASPARAGUS CLUB ROULADES 230
SALMON FILLETS STUFFED BY SEAFOOD 232
RACK OF LAMB 234
BEEF TENDERLOIN STUFFED BY ARTICHOKE 236
ROAST DUCKLING WITH CRANBERRY AND ORANGE 238
RAVIOLI WITH TOMATO SAUCE 240
TIKKA MASALA WITH CHICKEN 243
PORK TENDERLOIN WITH SPINACH 245
LEMONY SALMON PATTIES 248
BEEF CHUCK ROAST (SLOW-COOKER) 250
SHREDDED BARBECUE CHICKEN OVER GRITS 252
MUSHROOM-STUFFED FLANK STEAK ROLL 255
CLASSIC CRAB CAKES 258
SPAGHETTI MEATBALL SUPPER 260
PUFF PASTRY CHICKEN BUNDLES 263
TURKEY SAUSAGE-STUFFED ACORN SQUASH 265
CONCLUSION 268

INTRODUCTION

Tasty and Simple Menu Ideas answers questions such as:

- What can I cook that isn't too difficult but is still tasty?
- What can I cook that's quick and easy but not basic and bland?
- How can I please everyone in my family without preparing several different dishes?
- Where can I find delicious recipes with inexpensive ingredients?
- Where can I find recipes for healthy meals without following complicated diets?
- How can I create a varied weekly menu with many recipes?

This cookbook is intended for those who don't want to bother with "high cuisine," who aren't looking to lose weight or find exotic dishes, but who also don't want to eat convenience foods from the supermarket. This cookbook is for people who need to prepare quick and tasty meals for themselves or their families with products found in any American store.

My name is Alexandra Nichols. It's nice to meet you, reader! I love you all. I will be thrilled to read your comments. I am not a professional chef, but I am a certified nutritionist with many years of experience. Cooking is my passion. I devote a lot of time to it and do it with great pleasure. Creating not only tasty but also healthy food is an art. I invite each of you to evaluate my abilities to do this.

I wrote this book by recalling my experience at the beginning of my cooking journey. I remember how difficult it was for me to understand how to start cooking.

In this book, you will find effortless recipes, dishes that the whole family will enjoy, but that don't require standing for several hours at the stove. Also, a lack of kitchen skills is something that you must overcome before preparing any delicious food. To that end, my book is suitable for those who don't want to invest a lot of time to be able to eat delicious and healthy food every day. It's also for anyone who wants to learn how to cook proficiently but doesn't know how to start.

With this cookbook, you will feel that cooking is a fun and enjoyable process. You will learn that it can be easy to please your friends and family with home cooked meals. And this book is an excellent gift for family members or friends who want some help with their cooking but aren't looking to learn the secrets of haute cuisine.

Another obvious advantage of this book is the significant savings you'll get from preparing food at home.

When you cook at home, you are more likely to save money than when you buy the same type of food at a restaurant. Compare the classic chicken dinner with vegetables: the price of cooking it at home is 60 percent cheaper than eating at a restaurant. A simple chicken dinner costs six to eight dollars to make at home, more than thirteen dollars in the supermarket's prepared foods section, and more than fifteen dollars at a restaurant. Multiply these savings by the number of meals you eat in a month or a year to see how huge the savings truly are.

Finally, planning a diet can reduce food waste. Although it is nearly impossible to eliminate food waste, some simple planning techniques can significantly reduce it. For example, if I have some baby spinach leftover, I can try to plan a lunch or juice during the week that requires baby spinach. Eating only leftovers or planning to eat leftovers is a good trick for reducing food waste, which also saves you money!

When you read this book, by the next day, you will be able to prepare a delicious, healthy, and quick meal. I created this book to help you stop delaying your introduction to your kitchen.

More than one hundred simple and easy recipes for breakfast, lunch, dinner, and dessert for one, two, or even the whole family. No special appliances or exotic ingredients required. Each recipe includes a clear illustration.

The pages of this cookbook contain secrets that will make your life more comfortable and make cooking easier. Are you ready? Then let's get started!

Chapter 1 «MEAL PLANS»

Meal planning means taking some time to plan a given number of meals per week. Plan for yourself or your family. Plan a healthy diet. Plan all snacks or meals or just plan your lunch so you don't have to spend money in a restaurant that week. Just think about it: your plan can be basic. The goal is not to start from scratch with every meal. I think about meal plans and preparation for many reasons, but they can be divided into three categories.

Meal preparation is the meal planning and preparation process. This usually involves preparing food and cooking.

General food preparation requires the selection, measurement, and mixing of ingredients in an orderly procedure to achieve a desired result.

A meal plan can be defined as the time spent planning a nutritious meal for a specific period. This is the process of planning the type of food a family needs. When planning a healthy family diet, you must consider the type of food and incorporate nutrition in everyone's daily diet in a delicious way. Once a meal plan is made, you can purchase the ingredients corresponding to the meal specified in the plan.

A balanced diet consists of three meals each day representing the recommended daily quota for each food group. By ensuring that half of the food consumed daily is fruit and vegetables, and the other half is made of grains and protein with a small amount of low-fat dairy products, individuals can ensure a balanced and healthy diet.

FACTORS AFFECTING MEAL PLANS

Age of family members: The age of each family member affects their nutritional needs. These include children, teenagers, adults, and the elderly.

Family member's occupation or activity: A person's work will affect their nutritional needs. For example, manual workers need more energy from food than office workers.

Health status of family members: Some foods are not suitable for certain health conditions.

Family size: The family size determines the number of meals to be planned.

General season: Most foods are seasonal. Seasonal foods are cheaper, fresher, and tastier than non-seasonal ones. Provide different foods in different seasons.

Funding availability: The amount or type of food planned depends on household income.

Availability of time: Consider the time needed to prepare and serve meals.

MEAL PLAN TIPS

- The meal should contain all necessary nutrients.
- Provide food needs for all family members in the meal plan.
- Avoid monotonous foods and add variety.
- Make full use of food that is in season.
- Buy quality food.
- Plan meals a few days in advance to save money and time.

THE IMPORTANCE OF MEAL PLANS: THREE REASONS

TIME: This is the most attractive reason for me. I like to save time. Some people need to save more time than others. Everyone is different and everyone's needs are different. Choose a place where you need to save time and plan meals ahead. Simplify your diet or prepare in advance to help you later.

Breakfast: I am not a morning person at all. Breakfast is always the first thing I am late for, so I know that I need to prepare breakfast ahead of time and make it as easy as putting it in a microwave or toaster. If I plan in advance, then I can prepare a quick breakfast.

Lunch: If I don't have to run and find something to eat in the first half of the hour, my lunch break seems longer. Strange how preparing lunch saves so much time!

Dinner: If you plan ahead, you already know what dinner is and you already have the ingredients. My task is to provide you with the necessary information on how to prepare simple and tasty meals.

The importance of meal planning: the three reasons for planning meals every week are related to time, money, and our health. Here are some good arguments for using ProjectMealPlan.com for meal planning.

Most of the catering plan of the project focuses on preparing meals and things that can be done in advance to save future resources. This is because if you plan on eating, you can prepare food at any time, which saves more time. A meal plan can also save you time in the following ways:

Reduce grocery travel: If your weekly menu is pre-planned, then you can try your best to buy everything one week at a time.

Reduce roaming in the grocery store: I am a wanderer. Even with a list, sometimes I just want to search for sales or find delicious new products. But most of this is a waste of time.

Know what to prep: You know the list, so you know what to prepare. For example, we put chopped onions in almost everything. Therefore, instead of cutting them up into small pieces for each meal, we immediately chop everything all at once. You may not even think about it, but this can save three to four times the time it takes to clean and prep them individually. If I have time, I will also chop other vegetables. Save time by prepping food beforehand.

Plan leftovers: What can I say? I like leftovers. They save time because all you need to do is reheat them.

HEALTH: I am obviously not a health expert. However, this is my general idea of why meal plans are healthier than diet plans. Remember, everyone is different and everyone's needs are different. But when you plan ahead, you can make informed choices related to your personal health and fitness needs. This is why Project Meal Plan only provides an example of how to plan a person's meal based on preferences and needs. It can be done.

Here are some other insights about the importance of planning a healthy meal:

Eat the right amount: If I put it on a plate, I will eat it. Sometimes if you feel extremely hungry, happy, or just use spoons of different sizes, you can get completely different portions on the plate. Planning and pre-portioning food can ensure that your hard work is already done and you eat the right amounts.

Keep accountable: If you have already prepared the food and have it ready in consideration of future needs, then you will be less likely to eat something unhealthy at the last minute. Planning and preparing your meals can provide more motivation so that you can eat healthy food that has been planned and cooked.

More control over your choices: If you know you are eating out, you only need to plan. Eat light food for the rest of the day so you can enjoy it later. Do not indulge, only plan. Planning your choices in advance means you are more likely to stick to the healthy choices you have made.

MONEY: When you plan to cook, you are more likely to save money than buying the same type of food at a restaurant. Compare the classic chicken dinner with vegetables: the price of cooking it at home is 60% cheaper than eating at a restaurant. A simple chicken dinner costs $6 to $8 at home, more than $13 for meals, and more than $15 for meals outside. Multiply these savings by the number of meals you eat in a month or a year to see how huge the savings truly are. Finally, planning a diet can reduce food waste. Although it is almost impossible to eliminate waste 100%, some simple planning techniques can greatly reduce it. For example, if I have baby spinach leftover, I can try to plan a lunch or juice during the week that requires baby spinach. Eating only leftovers or planning to eat leftovers is a good habit for reducing food waste (and thus save money!).

THINGS TO REMEMBER ABOUT MEAL PLANNING

Don't let the long-term meal plan scare you. You can do anything as planned. You won't even have to cook. The important thing is that you have considered what you need and know what will happen.

Make your diet plan as flexible as possible. If you have a negative attitude towards meal plans because life can change and things happen, know that all that happens is that you deviate from the meal plan and learn from what happened. I would rather prepare more than I need than simply not prepare because things may change.

If you don't like eating the same thing every day, planning is especially important for you to save time and money and make healthy choices. You can cook a large amount of chicken or other meat for a week and eat it in different ways. Don't succumb to being picky, but work harder to find ideas that suits your needs. There are many articles on how to use one ingredient for different recipes.

Your ideal meal plan is in your mind—you only need a few resources. The point is to not have to start from scratch every night.

Chapter 2 «BREAKFAST RECIPES»

Breakfast is often eaten after a long break from food, as the time between dinner and breakfast ranges from 8-12 hours. Yet many people tend to skip this meal and do not start the day in a healthy or beneficial way.

THE BENEFITS OF BREAKFAST

Breakfast is one of the most important meals of the day, as studies have shown. It helps to provide the body with the energy it needs to complete the various actions necessary for the proper functioning of the brain and muscles. The following benefits include:

- Improved memory and focus
- Low levels of bad cholesterol (LDL)
- Controls blood sugar levels and lowers risk of diabetes
- Low risk of heart disease and blood pressure
- Improves physical performance and increases strength and endurance
- Helps with weight loss (if most daily calories are consumed in the morning)

Studies have shown that most people who lose weight and maintain a healthy weight eat breakfast regularly every day. As eating foods that contain protein and fiber in the morning help to control appetite for the rest of the day, it is not recommended to skip this meal in order to reduce calories. It is advised to choose foods carefully in a manner that takes into account the quantity, time, and health during breakfast, and that people who do not eat breakfast are more susceptible to obesity and related chronic diseases.

A healthy breakfast helps provide the body with the necessary vitamins and minerals that the body needs to grow properly and metabolizes nutrients such as protein and carbohydrates, in addition to maintaining bone strength and the immune system. People who regularly eat a healthy breakfast meet their daily nutritional needs and are more able to eat less fat.

THE IMPORTANCE OF BREAKFAST FOR CHILDREN

Eating breakfast is important for groups of all ages, but this applies especially to children and adolescents. As most children prefer not to eat in the morning, some simple foods can be prepared to eat on the way to school or between classes. These include fruits, nuts, and light sandwiches. The following points demonstrate the importance of not skipping breakfast for children and adolescents:

- ➢ A child's body needs nutrients and energy continually throughout the day as it is in a stage of rapid growth and development. It is worth noting that most children do not get all the vitamins and minerals they need from relying on lunch and dinner only.
- ➢ Skipping breakfast can cause fatigue.
- ➢ Some studies have shown that children who ate breakfast had higher test scores compared to children who did not.
- ➢ Studies have found that teenagers who ate breakfast had a lower BMI than those who did not eat it regularly, and children who did not eat breakfast were more likely to eat fast food during the day and gain weight.
- ➢ Breakfast helps improve athletic performance and physical activity, as well as improve focus levels, problem-solving skills, eye and hand coordination, creativity, and attention.

A HEALTHY BREAKFAST

Breakfast provides the opportunity to start the day with a healthy and nutritious meal and combines various health benefits, as it helps you to feel full for several hours. This meal can be prepared by choosing different foods from at least three food groups. It is worth noting that these groups provide the body with complex carbohydrates, fiber, protein, and a small amount of fat. To facilitate the process of preparing breakfast and not skip it, you can prepare it the night before. The following points show these groups:

Whole grains: oats, bread, cakes, breakfast cereals made with whole grains

Low-fat protein: eggs, lean meats, legumes, nuts

Low-fat dairy products: milk, yogurt, cheese

Fruits: fresh fruit such as apples, bananas, oranges, pears, peaches, and also dried fruit such as raisins and cranberries. These are easy to carry and consume outside the home. Frozen fruit can be used to make different juices naturally, but it is very important not to add sugar.

Fresh or frozen vegetables: can be added to sandwiches or scrambled eggs

IDEAS FOR MAKING HEALTHY BREAKFASTS

Simple and uncomplicated breakfasts can be prepared and do not take long. The following are some ideas for preparing a healthy breakfast:

Whipped cream made with fresh fruit

Smoothie: Blend half a cup of low-fat milk or yogurt, half a cup of orange juice with bananas, and 4-6 frozen strawberries. Possible additional ingredients: oats, peanut butter, cinnamon, vanilla extract, cocoa powder, mint, and instant coffee.

Peanut Butter Toast: Use whole wheat bread. Add the peanut butter and sliced bananas or apples.

Now you know more about breakfast and I want to share recipes for healthy, simple breakfasts that I prepare for myself and my family.

BREAKFAST FOR THE LAZY

Prep Time: 15 minutes

Servings: 3

INGREDIENTS
- Chicken egg 1 apiece
- Soft cottage cheese 7 oz.
- Wheat flour 1 oz.
- Sugar 1 tbsp

COOKING INSTRUCTIONS
1. Put the cottage cheese in a wide bowl. Add the eggs, sugar, and flour and mix with a fork until a homogeneous

consistency. If the mass is too sticky add more flour, but not more than half a tablespoon.

2. Sprinkle a little flour on the board and dump out the curd mass. Divide it into two equal parts and roll sausages of the same thickness from each.
3. Cut the sausages into small, identical slices with a sharp knife. If desired, you can slightly flatten each piece and give it a rounded shape.
4. In a small saucepan, bring the water to a boil. Gently lower the dumplings into boiling water one by one. Cook, stirring slightly with a slotted spoon, until all the dumplings float to the surface. Leave them for one more minute.
5. Place the prepared dumplings onto plates and serve with jam (for example, apricot). Serve them hot or warm.

RECIPE TIP

These lazy dumplings fully live up to their name. Even the biggest sloth will be able to arrange a great breakfast! Moreover, lazy dumplings can be served with any of your favorite toppings: honey, maple syrup, jam, fruit, anything your heart desires. At the very least, I hope you try them with sour cream or yogurt.

You can cook the dough in advance the night before and freeze it so that in the morning you just throw them into boiling water and not lose time on cooking.

BUCKWHEAT BREAKFAST

Prep Time: 1 hour 20 minutes
Servings: 4

INGREDIENTS

- Buckwheat 1 cup
- Minced parsley to taste
- Chopped cilantro to taste
- Chopped celery stalk to taste
- Lemon wedges
- Olive oil 2 tablespoons
- Soy sauce to taste

COOKING INSTRUCTIONS

1. Rinse the buckwheat. Pour 2 cups boiling water and salt over it. Cover with a towel.
After 45-60 minutes, buckwheat can be eaten without losing any nutritional value. This is preparation is best done the night before.
2. Place the required amount of steamed buckwheat in a bowl with olive oil, soy sauce, lemon juice, and chopped herbs. Mix.
3. Serve with chopped vegetables, such as bell peppers, carrots, pumpkin, and radishes. You can also serve it with a green smoothie.

RECIPE TIP

Buckwheat is the queen of cereals and the best doctor! There are more than enough trace elements in buckwheat. These include iron (promotes the formation of red blood cells and is responsible for a good complexion), potassium (maintains optimal blood pressure), calcium (your main ally in the fight against cavities, brittle nails, and brittle bones), magnesium (rescues you from depression and helps in the fight against excess weight), and many other minerals. It is an indispensable component of a healthy diet.

Buckwheat grains contain up to 16% easily-digestible proteins (including the essential amino acids arginine and lysine), up to 30% carbohydrates, and up to 3% of fats, as well as fiber; malic, citric, and oxalic acids; vitamin B, niacin, and bioflavonoids.

Doctors appreciate buckwheat for its large amount of rutin. This substance condenses the walls of blood vessels, stops bleeding, and has a preventive and therapeutic effect on veins (for example, varicose veins and hemorrhoids). In connective tissue, rutin strengthens the smallest blood vessels. Therefore, buckwheat porridge is extremely useful for various vascular diseases, rheumatic diseases, and arthritis. It improves blood circulation and strengthens the immune system.

Buckwheat porridge helps to remove excess cholesterol from the body (which means buckwheat lovers are not threatened with aging sclerosis and heart problems) and removes toxins and heavy metal ions as well, which is especially important for residents of large cities and areas with poor ecological conditions. Nutritionists recommend including buckwheat in the menu of patients with anemia, diabetes, and obesity. This is an indispensable dish for diseases of the nervous and cardiovascular systems, and abnormalities in the liver. Buckwheat is valued for its ability to maintain vision and cerebral circulation.

In general, it's not merely a porridge, but a real natural pharmacy. Buckwheat can easily be used as an alternative to medicines. Do not buy the fried cereal, but buckwheat that is pale yellow in color. Remember that in order for buckwheat to retain all its useful properties, it must be properly cooked.

FRENCH BREAKFAST

Prep Time: 15 minutes

Servings: 3

INGREDIENTS
- White bread 3 pieces
- Milk ½ cup
- Banana ½
- Crushed cardamom 1 tbsp

COOKING INSTRUCTIONS
1. Mix milk, cardamom, and banana pulp in a blender.

2. Dip slices of bread or rolls in the resulting mixture on both sides and fry in a pan or bake in the oven 350 degrees F for about 10 minutes.

LOW-CALORIE BREAKFAST

Prep Time: 10 minutes

Servings: 1

INGREDIENTS

- Green salad0 1 leaf (more to taste)
- Chicken egg 1 apiece
- Tomato ½
- Ramson 3 stems
- Russian cheese 1 oz.
- Salt to taste

COOKING INSTRUCTION

1. Hard-boil the egg. Cut cheese and tomatoes.
2. Mix the ingredients.
3. Salt to taste.

RECIPE TIP
This breakfast is high in protein and has virtually no carbohydrates.

FRENCH CROUTONS FOR BREAKFAST

Prep Time: 10 minutes

Servings: 1

INGREDIENTS
- Baton bread 3 pieces
- Milk 2 tablespoons
- Chicken egg 1 apiece
- Salt to taste
- Vegetable oil 1 tablespoon

COOKING INSTRUCTIONS
1. Mix the egg with milk. Salt to taste.
2. Dip slices of loaf in egg mixture on both sides.
3. Fry in vegetable oil on both sides.

CURD BUNS FOR BREAKFAST

Prep Time: 20 minutes

Servings: 8

INGREDIENTS
- Chicken eggs 2
- Sugar 3 tablespoons
- Salt pinch
- Vanilla sugar 1 teaspoon
- Baking powder ½ oz.
- Milk 2 tablespoons

- Wheat flour 8 ½ oz.
- Soft cottage cheese 8 ½ oz.

COOKING INSTRUCTIONS

1. Stir the cottage cheese, eggs, sugar, vanilla sugar, and salt with a whisk until smooth. Sift flour with baking powder and knead soft, sticky dough.
2. Cover the baking sheet with baking paper and grease with sunflower oil.
3. Wet buns with wet hands, place on a baking sheet, and bake in a preheated oven at 350 degrees F for about 12 minutes.
4. Remove the buns, brush with milk. You may sprinkle a little sugar over them and place them in the oven again for 3-5 minutes or until brown.

PEASANT BREAKFAST

Prep Time: 40 minutes

Servings: 4

INGREDIENTS
- Boiled sausage 3 1/2 oz.
- Smoked loin 3 1/2 oz.
- Bulb onions 2 5/8 oz.
- Chicken eggs 7
- Milk 100 ml
- Potatoes 8
- Butter 1 3/4 oz.
- Salted cucumbers 7 oz.

- Chives 1 oz.
- Salt to taste

COOKING INSTRUCTIONS

1. Cut the loin, sausage, and peeled onions into cubes and fry.
2. Boil the potatoes, peel and cut into slices, fry in butter. Put everything together in a pan.
3. Mix the eggs with milk, beat slightly, salt, and pour the mixture into a pan with the potatoes and sausage. Place in a heated 350 degree F oven and bake for about 30 minutes.
4. When serving, sprinkle with chopped green onions. Serve pickles separately.

POTATO AND HAM SLICES FOR BREAKFAST

Prep Time: 30 minutes

Servings: 2

INGREDIENTS
- Chives 3 stems
- Hard cheese 3 ½ oz.
- Salt to taste
- Potatoes 4
- Ham 5 ¼ oz.
- Ground black pepper to taste

- Chicken eggs 2
- Wheat flour 1 tablespoon

COOKING INSTRUCTIONS
1. Grate potatoes, ham and cheese.
2. Add raw eggs, green onions, pepper, and (if necessary) salt.
3. Add flour and mix well.
4. Roll in flour, shape in the form of meatballs, and fry them in a pan.
5. Serve with sour cream.

LUSH PANCAKES FOR BREAKFAST

Prep Time: 25 minutes

Servings: 4

INGREDIENTS
- Kefir 1 cup
- Water 40 ml
- Chicken egg 1
- Wheat flour 10 5/8 oz.
- Sugar 3 tablespoons
- Salt 1 tsp
- Soda 1/4 tbsp

COOKING INSTRUCTIONS

1. Mix kefir with water and warm slightly.
2. Turn off the heat and add salt, sugar, and egg. Stir well until foam appears on top.
3. Add flour, mix thoroughly so that there are no lumps. It should become a thick mass.
4. After the batter is ready, add soda and again mix thoroughly.
5. Fry over medium heat.

STRAWBERRY BREAKFAST

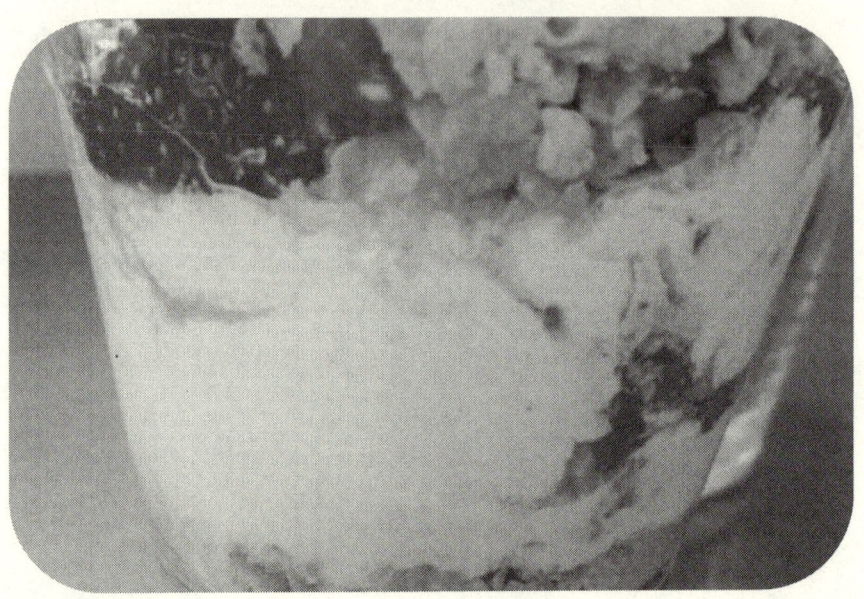

Prep Time: 5 minutes

Servings: 1

INGREDIENTS
- Strawberry 5.3 oz.
- Strawberry yogurt 100 g (more to taste)
- Cornflakes 2.5 oz.

COOKING INSTRUCTIONS
1. Dice the strawberries.
2. Pour half the strawberry into a glass.
3. Add half of the yogurt.
4. Add half the cereal.

5. Repeat one more time.

RECIPE TIP
Cornflakes can be replaced with muesli. Instead of strawberry yogurt, use any other you prefer. If desired, mix yogurt with a teaspoon of sugar.

EGG SALSA SANDWICHE

Prep Time: 25 minutes

Servings: 4

INGREDIENTS
- 8 large eggs
- 1/2 teaspoon salt
- 1/4 teaspoon pepper
- 1 cup salsa, divided
- 1/2 cup shredded cheddar cheese
- 4 whole wheat English muffins, split and toasted
- 1/4 cup reduced-fat spreadable cream cheese

- 1 medium ripe avocado, peeled and cubed
- 1/2 small lime
- Reduced-fat sour cream, optional

COOKING INSTRUCTIONS

1. In a large bowl, whisk eggs, salt and pepper. Place a large nonstick skillet coated with cooking spray over medium-high heat. Pour in egg mixture; cook and stir until eggs are thickened and no liquid egg remains. Add 1/2 cup salsa and cheese; stir gently until cheese is melted.
2. Spread cut sides of English muffins with cream cheese and remaining salsa. Top with scrambled eggs and avocado. Squeeze lime juice over tops. If desired, serve with sour cream.

HEALTHY BREAKFAST

Prep Time: 10 minutes

Servings: 1

INGREDIENTS
- Oats 1 tablespoon
- Flax seeds 1 tablespoon
- Cranberry 3.5 oz.

COOKING INSTRUCTIONS
1. Place all ingredients in a thermos, pour in 1/2 cup boiling water, and leave overnight.
2. In the morning, grind steamed cereals with a blender until smooth. Add a banana if desired.

POTATO PANKECES

Prep Time: 30 minutes

Servings: 2

INGREDIENTS
- 4 cups shredded peeled potatoes (about 4 large potatoes)
- 1 large egg, lightly beaten
- 3 tablespoons all-purpose flour
- 1 tablespoon grated onion
- 1 teaspoon salt
- 1/4 teaspoon pepper
- Oil for frying
- Optional: Chopped parsley, applesauce and sour cream

COOKING INSTRUCTIONS

1. Rinse shredded potatoes in cold water; drain well, squeezing to remove excess water. Place in a large bowl. Stir in egg, flour, onion, salt and pepper.
2. In a large nonstick skillet, heat 1/4 in. oil over medium heat. Working in batches, drop potato mixture by 1/3 cupfuls into oil; press to flatten slightly. Fry both sides until golden brown; drain on paper towels. Serve immediately. If desired, sprinkle with parsley and top with applesauce and sour cream.

CURD AND HONEY OR BREAKFAST FOR YOURSELF

Prep Time: 5 minutes

Servings: 1

INGREDIENTS
- Honey 3 tablespoons
- Soft cottage cheese 3.5 oz.
- Prunes 7
- Jam 2 tablespoons

COOKING INSTRUCTIONS
1. Take a beautiful plate, preferably dark. Place large cut prunes on the plate.

2. Put the cottage cheese on top.
3. Next, drizzle with honey.
4. Place more prunes on top.
5. If desired, add jam.

RECIPE TIP
For me, cottage cheese can be completely fat-free or with a fat content of two percent. Lumps are less likely to occur in low-fat cottage cheese.

Growing up, there was often a jar of mashed feijoa or blackcurrant at home, so I got used to their tastes. But sometimes blueberry or strawberry jam are good options. Add only a little on top or it will be too sweet. Better yet, if there are fresh strawberries, then add those too.

About prunes: their presence at the bottom of the dish is very important. You can't imagine how tasty it is to accidentally find it inside a spoon with cottage cheese and honey and already in your mouth!

And of course, serve it with a favorite cup of coffee. I won't even mention that it should be natural.

FRIED EGG WITH ZUCCHINI FOR BREAKFAST

Prep Time: 10 minutes

Servings: 1

INGREDIENTS
- Zucchini 1
- Chicken egg 1
- Salt to taste
- Mixture of peppers to taste
- Vegetable oil 1 tablespoon

COOKING INSTRUCTIONS
1. Cut the zucchini into very thin strips.

2. Put them in hot oil in a frying pan. Fry over medium heat for 2 minutes, stirring constantly so as not to burn.

3. Break the egg into the pan, season with salt and pepper. Cover, cook for another 5–8 minutes (depending on the desired egg consistency). Serve immediately.

SCRAMBLED EGGS FOR BREAKFAST

Prep Time: 5 minutes

Servings: 2

INGREDIENTS
- Chicken eggs 6
- Cream 25% ¼ cup
- Butter 0.5 oz.
- Salt to taste
- Freshly ground black pepper taste
- Chives to taste

COOKING INSTRUCTIONS

1. Beat eggs in a bowl with cream for about 1 minute until smooth. Salt the mixture and beat lightly again.
2. Melt the butter in a pan over medium heat. The butter should completely cover the bottom. When it begins to bubble, pour the mixture into the pan.
3. Reduce the heat slightly. When the mixture begins to set, start mixing it to the center with a wooden spoon for about 1-2 minutes until tender.
4. Sprinkle with freshly ground black pepper and the chives before serving.

CHEESECAKES FOR BREAKFAST

Prep Time: 30 minutes

Servings: 4

INGREDIENTS
- Cottage cheese 1.3 oz.
- Chicken egg 1
- Sugar 1 tablespoon
- Wheat flour ½ cup

COOKING INSTRUCTIONS
1. Mix all the ingredients together.

2. Roll the sausage shape from the resulting dough, cut into thin circles.

3. Roll the future cheesecakes in flour.

4. Fry in vegetable oil for 2-3 minutes on each side until golden brown.

CURD BREAKFAST WITH MANGO AND ORANGE

Prep Time: 10 minutes

Servings: 1

INGREDIENTS
- Mango 1
- Cottage cheese 3.5 oz.
- Oranges 2

COOKING INSTRUCTIONS

1. Peel, cut, and toss the mango into a blender. Peel the oranges, squeeze 1.5 oranges with your hands into the blender. Toss in the remaining half as is.
2. Blend everything.
3. Put the cottage cheese in a deep plate and pour the resulting mixture on top. Stir with a spoon as desired.

TAMAGOYAKI FOR BREAKFAST

Prep Time: 20 minutes

Servings: 1

INGREDIENTS
- Chicken eggs 4
- Soy sauce 1 teaspoon
- Sugar 1.5 teaspoons
- Dry white wine to taste
- Vegetable oil to taste
- Salt to taste

COOKING INSTRUCTIONS

1. First, beat the eggs with a whisk. Don't use a mixer since it will create unnecessary foam. Filter the mixture through a sieve—it should be completely homogeneous, without pieces of unmixed protein.

2. Add the remaining ingredients: sugar, salt, wine, and soy sauce. Stir until sugar is completely dissolved. Instead of wine, you can add rice vinegar.

3. Pour a little egg mixture into a preheated small diameter pan. Get a thin pancake. Make sure that it does not bubble. If this happens, we puncture the bubbles and reduce the heat. Most likely it happens because the pan is too hot.

4. When the bottom is properly fried, begin to tightly roll the omelet with a spatula or chop sticks. Place the roll to the side of the pan.

5. Repeat step 3, including the first roll inside the new roll. Do this about four more times.

6. Inside the omelet, you can pre-add the filling. This involves placing it on top of the thin egg pancake before you roll it.

FRUIT BREAKFAST WITH NUTS

Prep Time: 10 minutes

Servings: 2

INGREDIENTS
- Bananas 2
- Walnuts 8.8 oz.
- Apple 1

COOKING INSTRUCTIONS
1. Cut the apple into small cubes.
2. Crush the peeled nuts, mix with the apple.

3. Puree the banana in a blender and pour over the apples and nuts.

APPLE AND OAT SMOOTHIE FOR BREAKFAST

Prep Time: 10 minutes

Servings: 2

INGREDIENTS
- Oatmeal 3 tablespoons
- Apple 1
- Vanilla extract ¼ teaspoon

- Almond milk 1 cup
- Sugar to taste

COOKING INSTRUCTIONS

1. First add oatmeal to the blender and grind to flour consistency.
2. Add the remaining ingredients and mix until smooth. Serve immediately.

KHACHAPURI FOR BREAKFAST

Prep Time: 30 minutes

Servings: 1

INGREDIENTS
- Cheese 10.6 oz.
- Milk 1 cup
- Wheat flour 1 cup
- Chicken egg 1

COOKING INSTRUCTIONS
1. Combine the egg, milk. and flour in a bowl. Beat well.

2. Grate the cheese or mash the cottage cheese, depending on what you cook khachapuri with.

3. Pour cheese (cottage cheese) into the dough.

4. Stir well.

5. Pour the resulting mass into a pan. After some time, turn over (after about 10 minutes). When the khachapuri is browned, remove from heat.

6. Serve hot.

CROUTONS WITH TOMATOES AND CHEESE FOR BREAKFAST

Prep Time: 20 minutes

Servings: 4

INGREDIENTS
- White bread 3 pieces
- Chicken egg 1
- Milk 2 tablespoons
- Tomatoes halved
- Grated cheese 3 tablespoons

- Vegetable oil to taste
- Dill to taste
- Salt to taste
- Ground black pepper to taste

COOKING INSTRUCTIONS

1. Mix the egg with the milk, chopped dill, salt, and pepper. Beat the whole mixture well with a whisk or a fork.
2. Cut the bread. Put slices of bread in the egg mixture and let it soak well.
3. Place a frying pan with vegetable oil on the stove and warm it up.
4. Fry the croutons on both sides. If a little egg mixture remains in the plate, then gently add it over the croutons.
5. Place a thin slice of tomato on the prepared croutons, lightly salt and pepper.
6. Sprinkle with grated cheese and grill until tender so that the cheese melts and forms a beautiful crust.

RAISIN BUNS FOR BREAKFAST

Prep Time: 35 minutes

Servings: 3

INGREDIENTS
- Wheat flour 4 cups
- Water 300 ml
- Raisins 6.7 oz.
- Sugar 1 tablespoon
- Dry yeast 0.2 oz.

COOKING INSTRUCTIONS
1. Combine flour, sugar, and yeast.
2. Knead a thick dough.
3. Add raisins to the dough.
4. Form buns, let rest for 10 minutes.
5. Bake on parchment paper for about 20 minutes over high heat in a in a 350 degrees F preheated oven.

RECIPE TIP
Serve for breakfast with honey and coffee.

BREAKFAST CAKE WITH EGGS AND SAUSAGE

Prep Time: 30 minutes

Servings: 1

INGREDIENTS
- Chicken egg 1
- Sour cream 1 tablespoon
- Salt to taste
- Sausage 1.8 oz.
- Cheese to taste
- Green onions to taste
- Wheat flour 1 tablespoon

COOKING INSTRUCTION

1. Chop green onions and sausage finely.
2. Beat the eggs.
3. Add sour cream and stir.
4. Stir everything: flour, salt, green onions, sausage.
5. Fry like pancakes on both sides in a hot pan.
6. When the cakes are ready, grate the cheese on top and fold in half.
7. Serve hot.

CHAPTER 3
«DESSERT RECIPES»

Dessert is a beautiful meal. The course usually consists of sweets and may also include beverages such as candy liquor or liqueur. However, in the United States, this may include coffee, cheese, nuts, or other delicious ingredients, which are considered separate packages elsewhere.

HEALTHY DESSERTS

A person can eat sweets, but the types with the lowest fat and sugar content, rich in nutrients (such as vitamins, minerals, and fiber) must be chosen. Also take care of preparing them in a healthy way, and this can be easily done by adding fruit. It is considered a healthy source of sugar and can be eaten alone or added to sweets and can also be added to milk. You can also add nuts, honey, or dark chocolate. Other examples of healthy sweets include:

- Banana with ice cream and peanut butter
- Fruit salad
- Carrot cake with oats

WAYS TO MAKE DESSERT HEALTHY

Dessert recipes can be prepared in a healthy way and some of these tips include the following:

➢ Try to skip steps to that require adding butter or oil, reduce the amounts, or use healthier substitutes such as apple sauce. This may help to reduce fat and calories.
➢ Prepare desserts using a third or half of the amount of sugar called for in the recipe.
➢ Use milk in desserts instead of sugars and processed cream.

PINEAPPLE WITH LIME AND HONEY

INGREDIENTS
- Pineapple 10.6 oz.
- Limes 2
- Honey 1 teaspoon

COOKING INSTRUCTIONS
1. Peel the chilled pineapple and slice thinly. Squeeze the juice from the limes and whisk it together with honey. Pour the sauce over the pineapple slices and let it lightly marinate for five minutes. This pineapple can be a dessert or a side dish for shrimp.

NO-BAKE CURD DESSERT

Prep Time: 20 minutes

Servings: 4

INGREDIENTS
- Soft cottage cheese 17.6 oz.
- Sour cream 10% 10.6 oz.
- Gelatin 1.1 oz.
- Sugar to taste
- Fruit to taste

COOKING INSTRUCTIONS

1. Mix the cottage cheese and sour cream until smooth.
2. Add sugar or honey to taste.
3. Pour gelatin into a glass of water and let set for 10 minutes. Then heat over a slow fire, not bringing to a boil but stirring constantly. Wait until the gelatin is completely dissolved in water.
4. Pour gelatin into the curd/sour cream mass in a thin stream and mix thoroughly. Obtain a liquid mass.
5. Put your favorite fruits or berries in the bottom of the mold. Pour the resulting mixture over it and set in the refrigerator for 1-2 hours.
6. When serving, you can decorate with syrup, a sprig of mint, and berries.

RECIPE TIP

It is better to use soft cottage cheese. It's easier to mix with sour cream, and the consistency is tender, without lumps. Sour cream, if desired, can be replaced with yogurt.

NO-BAKE SWEDISH DESSERT (CHOKLADBOLLAR)

Prep Time: 30 minutes
Servings: 7

INGREDIENTS
- Sugar 2 cups
- Butter 5.3 oz.
- Vanilla sugar 1.5 tablespoons
- Cocoa powder 4.5 tablespoons
- Coconut flakes 1 cup

- Instant oat flakes 3.5 cups
- Strong coffee 3 tablespoons

COOKING INSTRUCTIONS

1. Wait until the oil reaches room temperature.
2. Beat butter with sugar with a mixer (or mix well by hand).
3. Add vanilla sugar and cocoa, mix.
4. Grind oatmeal in a blender, add to the mixture. Include coffee (if you use instant, dissolve 2-3 teaspoons of coffee in 2 tablespoons of hot water). Mix.
5. Roll the balls from the resulting mixture with a tablespoon. Roll them in coconut flakes. Chill before serving.

RECIPE TIP

From these specific ingredients, you can make 14 balls. Keep refrigerated. Chokladbollars are perfectly stored in the freezer. Instead of coffee, you can use orange juice or water.

NO-BAKE BERRY FRUIT DESSERT

Prep Time: 30 minutes

Servings: 8

INGREDIENTS
- Butter 2.1 oz.
- Cookies 5.3 oz.
- Gelatin 1 tablespoon
- Strawberry yogurt 5.3 oz.
- Sugar ½ cup
- Frozen berries 17.6 oz.
- Cream 7.1 oz.

COOKING INSTRUCTIONS

1. Crumb cookies in a blender and mix with butter. Place the dough in a mold (about 22 cm in diameter) and let it rest in the refrigerator.
2. Defrost berries, drain the juice. Dilute gelatin in the juice, allow it to swell for 30–40 minutes and warm up to complete dissolution (do not bring to a boil!).
3. Add sugar to the berries, slightly grind in the blender. Mix with yogurt, add gelatin, wait for it to set a little, and pour into the mold with the base.
4. Allow to freeze in the refrigerator.
5. For a more festive option, you can whip 200 ml of cream (at least 30%) and add into the soufflé after gelatin. The taste will be even more creamy.

NO-BAKE ALMOND APRICOT DESSERT

Prep Time: 20 minutes

Servings: 10

INGREDIENTS
- Ground almonds 12 oz.
- Sugar ¾ cup
- Egg white 7
- Powdered sugar 3 cups
- Almond essence ⅓ teaspoon
- Apricot jam 3 tablespoons
- Lemon juice ½ cup

- Gelatin 2 teaspoons
- Apricots 6

COOKING INSTRUCTIONS

1. Grind the almonds and mix with ¾ cup sugar and ¾ cup powdered sugar. Add 3 egg whites, the almond essence, and knead the dough. Divide the dough into three parts.
2. Roll out one part on a surface sprinkled with sugar. Create the high sides from the rest of the dough. Lubricate the bottom and sides of the cake with apricot jam. Leave the cake to dry for at least 3 days before putting the filling in.
3. Place the peeled apricot halves on the dried cake. Beat egg whites, gradually adding powdered sugar. Then add lemon juice and glycerin and beat again. Put the finished dessert in the refrigerator for 1 day.

THIN PANCAKES IN MILK

Prep Time: 40 minutes

Servings: 4

INGREDIENTS
- Wheat flour 1.4 oz.
- Sugar 2 tablespoons
- Chicken eggs 4
- Milk 1 liter
- Salt on the tip of a knife
- Vegetable oil 2 tablespoons

COOKING INSTRUCTIONS
1. Beat eggs with sugar.

2. Gradually introduce flour and salt, alternating with milk, and gently stir until smooth.
3. Leave for 20 minutes.
4. Add vegetable oil to the dough and fry the pancakes in a very hot pan.

CLASSIC CHARLOTTE

Prep Time: 35 minutes

Servings: 12

INGREDIENTS
- Sugar 1 cup
- Chicken eggs 5
- Wheat flour 1 cup
- Apples 7
- Vegetable oil 1 tablespoon
- Slaked soda ½ teaspoon

COOKING INSTRUCTIONS

1. Preheat the oven. Separate the whites and beat them into a strong foam, gradually adding sugar.
2. Continue to beat, adding one yolk, then slaked soda and flour. The consistency of the dough should resemble sour cream.
3. Lubricate the pan with vegetable oil. Pour half the dough onto a baking sheet, spread the sliced apples evenly, pour out the second half of the dough.
4. Place the pan in a preheated oven. Hold for 3 minutes at a temperature of 400 degrees F, then reduce to 350 degrees F and bake for 20-25 minutes.

BLUEBERRY AND NUTMEG MUFFINS

Prep Time: 35 minutes

Servings: 12

INGREDIENTS
- Butter 3.9 oz.
- Wheat flour 10.2 oz.
- Baking powder 2 teaspoons
- Salt pinch
- Sugar 8.8 oz.
- Blueberries 1 cup

- Chicken eggs 2
- Vanilla extract 2 teaspoons
- Milk 120 ml
- Nutmeg ¼ teaspoon

COOKING INSTRUCTIONS

1. Grease the muffin pan with butter and sprinkle with flour.
2. With a whisk, mix flour, salt, and baking powder. Roll the blueberries in two teaspoons of the flour mixture.
3. Using a mixer, beat the butter and sugar (200 grams) at medium speed. It takes about four to five minutes. Then add eggs one at a time, then vanilla.
4. Switch the mixer to the slowest mode, add flour, stir, and gradually pour in the milk. It is necessary to stir until the dough is more or less mixed through, then the muffins will turn out tender and loose. Use a spatula to stir in the blueberries.
5. Pour the dough into molds. Mix the remaining 50 grams of sugar with grated nutmeg and sprinkle the tops of the muffins.
6. Put the muffins in an oven preheated to 380 degrees F and bake for about 25 minutes.

RECIPE TIP
Blueberries can be replaced with cranberries or raspberries. The berries may well be frozen, but the main thing is not to defrost them in advance and put them directly in the dough, otherwise they will release a lot of water and the muffins will become soggy.

CARROT CUPCAKES WITH GINGER AND CINNAMON

Prep Time: 1 hour

Servings: 12

INGREDIENTS
- Carrots 4
- Wheat flour 1.5 cups
- Baking powder 1.5 teaspoons
- Ground cinnamon 1 teaspoon
- Soda ½ teaspoon
- Nutmeg ¼ teaspoon
- Ground ginger ½ teaspoon

- Vegetable oil ¾ cup
- Soft brown sugar 1 cup
- Chicken eggs 3
- Vanilla extract 1 teaspoon
- Salt ¾ teaspoon

COOKING INSTRUCTIONS

1. Grate carrots (4 medium size) with a coarse grater.
2. Mix flour, baking powder, soda, salt, cinnamon, ginger, and nutmeg.
3. Beat together the butter, eggs, and brown sugar with a mixer at high speed. Add grated carrots and vanilla to the creamy mass and mix until a homogeneous consistency. Then pour in the flour mixture in parts and bring it to a dough state with a mixer at low speed.
4. Put parchment paper inserts into the cupcake tray and place the dough in them.
5. Bake in a preheated oven at 380 degrees F for about 20-25 minutes.
6. After they bake, leave the prepared cupcakes for 10 minutes to cool, then remove them along with the paper and allow to cool for at least 1 hour. Sprinkle with powdered sugar before serving.

OATMEAL RAISIN COOKIES WITH SESAME SEEDS

Prep Time: 25 minutes

Servings: 12

INGREDIENTS
- Honey 1.8 oz.
- Vegetable oil 50 ml
- Cinnamon 1/3 teaspoon
- Lemon 1

- Ginger root 0.5 oz.
- Instant oatmeal 7.1 oz.
- Wheat flour 3.5 oz.
- Sesame seeds 1.1 oz.
- Walnuts 1.8 oz.
- Raisins 1.4 oz.

COOKING INSTRUCTIONS

1. Preheat the oven to 350 degrees F. Finely chop raisins and walnuts.
2. Grate ginger.
3. In a small pot, heat the juice of one lemon, the zest of half a lemon, honey, cinnamon, and grated ginger.
4. Pour oatmeal, nuts, raisins, and sesame seeds into a bowl. Add vegetable oil, flour, and the warmed syrup of the honey, lemon juice, and spices. Knead the dough.
5. Then, with a tablespoon or your hands, form cookies and place them on a baking sheet that's been covered with parchment paper.
6. Bake for about 15 minutes. Allow the cookies to cool before serving.

RECIPE TIP
You can add different nuts. The more nut combinations, the tastier the cookies. For example, walnuts can be combined with almonds or sunflower seeds.

COTTAGE CHEESE DONUTS IN ICING SUGAR

Prep Time: 40 minutes

Servings: 4

INGREDIENTS
- Cottage cheese 8.8 oz.
- Chicken eggs 3
- Wheat flour 8 tablespoons
- Sugar 3 tablespoons
- Salt ½ teaspoon
- Olive oil to taste

- Soda ½ teaspoon
- Powdered vanilla sugar to taste

COOKING INSTRUCTIONS

1. Put the cottage cheese in a clean bowl, add eggs, flour, sugar, soda, and salt. Mix everything gently with a spatula or wooden spoon until smooth.
2. Pour olive (or vegetable) oil into a small stewpan so that at least half of the donut can be immersed. Heat oil well.
3. Using a teaspoon or your hands, roll balls from the dough, each a little smaller than a walnut. Periodically dip them in flour so that the dough does not stick to your hands.
4. Throw donuts into boiling oil and fry over low heat, constantly turning over with a slotted spoon so that they brown evenly on all sides and acquire a beautiful golden brown hue.
5. Put the finished donuts on a paper towel and leave for one to two minutes so that excess oil is absorbed. Serve the donuts hot by placing them on a dish and sprinkling with powdered sugar mixed with vanilla.

RECIPE TIP

Olive oil for frying should be the refined and deodorized variety, with a neutral taste and smell. If this is not at hand, you can use sunflower oil, also refined and odorless.

TRADITIONAL NAPOLEON CAKE

Prep Time: 4 hours

Servings: 12

INGREDIENTS
- Wheat flour 6 cups
- Butter 18 oz.
- Oil 0.5 oz.
- Water 200 ml
- Salt ½ teaspoon
- Milk 3 l

- Sugar 17.6 oz.
- Chicken eggs 5
- Vanillin 0.4 oz.

COOKING INSTRUCTIONS

1. Pour 6 cups of flour onto the work surface for the dough. Put 18 oz. of butter in the flour and chop finely with a knife to combine it. Form dough from this mass.
2. Mix cold but not icy water with salt and gradually pour into the center of the dough, constantly mixing the whole mass. When all the water is poured in, mix thoroughly to make a uniform dough.
3. Divide the dough into 9 equal parts. Roll cakes with a maximum thickness of 2 mm onto a surface sprinkled with flour, and bake for 15–20 minutes in an oven preheated to 350 degrees F.
4. For cream, heat 2.5 liters of milk.
5. While the milk is boiling, place the eggs and sugar in a bowl. Add flour to the mass and mix everything thoroughly. After that, pour in the remaining milk (0.5 liters) and mix until smooth.
6. When the milk is heated well, pour the egg mass into it in a thin stream, stirring continuously. Continuing to stir, bring the cream to a boil and turn off immediately, as bubbles appear on the surface. Add 0.5 oz. of oil and

vanillin to the hot cream. If desired, you can add more sugar.

7. Build the cake on a dish, generously smearing each layer with cream. There is a lot of cream so do not skimp; let it flow down the sides so the cake is well-saturated. Crumble one layer and sprinkle it over the top and sides of the finished cake.

8. Let the cake set, and after 6-7 hours you can enjoy!

RECIPE TIP
With 9 cakes, each of them will turn out to be about 30 cm in diameter. Therefore, if you want to make the cake smaller, divide the dough into more parts so the cake will grow in height, not in width. When you divide the dough, keep the pieces in the refrigerator and take out one portion each to roll out. Since the dough contains a lot of oil, it will become too soft at room temperature and you will not be able to roll it out. Allow the finished cream to cool slightly before frosting the cakes.

GINGER COOKIES WITH VANILLA SUGAR

Prep Time: 20 minutes
Servings: 8

INGREDIENTS
- Ginger root 1
- Wheat flour 5.6 oz.
- Butter 2.7 oz.
- Brown sugar 2.8 oz.
- Vanilla sugar 0.5 oz.

- Egg yolk 1
- Gingerbread spice mix 1 teaspoon
- Baking powder 1 teaspoon
- Salt pinch

COOKING INSTRUCTIONS

1. Wash, peel, and grate the ginger root. Only 2 teaspoons of grated ginger are needed for cookies.
2. In a mixer at high speed, mix cold butter diced into large cubes with brown sugar and a pinch of salt, then add the egg yolk and mix again.
3. Sift the flour along with vanilla sugar, baking powder, and gingerbread spice. Add this mixture and grated ginger to the wet ingredients in the mixer, gradually and in small portions. Kneading the dough is better with a mixer rather than with your hands: you should not overheat the shortbread dough. If you combine the dough with your hands, and it will be too hard. Ready dough should be put in the refrigerator for an hour.
4. Roll the chilled dough with a rolling pin in all directions to a thickness of 1.5 mm. Using cookie cutters, cut out the figured cookies. Transfer them to a baking sheet lined with parchment paper and place in the oven preheated to 360 degrees F for 5 to 8 minutes—until the edges of the cookies begins to brown.

TSVETAEVA APPLE PIE

Prep Time: 30 minutes

Servings: 4

INGREDIENTS
- An Apple 18 oz.
- Wheat flour 2 cups
- Sour cream 1.5 cups
- Butter 5.3 oz.
- Slaked vinegar 1 teaspoon
- Sugar 1 cup
- Soda ½ teaspoon
- Chicken egg 1

COOKING INSTRUCTIONS

1. Grate the room temperature butter and mix with 1.5 cups of flour. Then pour half a glass of sour cream into the dough and mix well. At the end, add the slaked vinegar to the soda. Mix and slightly knead the dough with your hands. The dough should turn out soft and not stick.
2. Peel the apples, remove the core, and use a potato peeler to cut into thin slices similar to petals.
3. Roll out the dough and give it the shape of the dish in which you will bake the pie. Lay the dough on the bottom of the dish, lay the apple petals on top.
4. In a separate bowl, mix 1 cup sour cream, egg, sugar, and 2 tablespoons of flour and beat slightly. The cream should be quite liquid in consistency. Fill the mold with dough and apple cream.
5. Preheat the oven to 390 degrees F and bake for 50 minutes.

"PIGEON'S MILK" CAKE

Prep Time: 1 hour 40 minutes
Servings: 10

INGREDIENTS
- Wheat flour 4.9 oz.
- Butter 12.4 oz.
- Sugar 14.1 oz.
- Chicken eggs 2
- Chocolate 2.7 oz.
- Condensed milk 3.5 oz.
- Egg white 2.1 oz.

- Citric acid ½ teaspoon
- Vanilla extract 2 ml
- Agar-agar 0.1 oz.

COOKING INSTRUCTIONS

1. Soak agar-agar in 140 ml of water for two to three hours. Beat 100 grams of butter and the same amount of sugar. Add eggs, 1 ml of vanilla extract, beat to a homogeneous consistency. Pour flour into the resulting white mass and knead the dough.

2. Line two baking sheets with baking paper, put the dough in two circles the size of a cake mold. Bake cakes at 390 degrees F for ten minutes, trim the edges. Cool the cakes without removing from the paper.

3. Beat condensed milk and 7.1 oz. of room temperature oil in a cream, add 1 ml of vanilla extract and set aside (not in the refrigerator).

4. Bring water with agar-agar over low heat to a boil, continuously stirring with a spatula. Boil for a minute, add 10.6 oz. of sugar. Increase heat to medium, bring the syrup to a boil again, and cook for a couple of minutes, stirring occasionally. The consistency can be checked by tearing the surface of the syrup—a thin thread should stretch behind it. Let the syrup cool.

5. Beat the cooled proteins until stable, add citric acid, beat the proteins in a dense mass. Pour hot syrup into it with a thin stream (the protein mass will greatly increase in volume). Beat to density and mix with condensed oil at low speed with a mixer. As soon as the consistency becomes homogeneous, the soufflé is ready.
6. Put the first cake in the cake mold, pour half of the soufflé from above. Cover it with a second cake, fill with the remaining soufflé. Put the cake in the refrigerator for three to four hours to freeze the soufflé.
7. Melt the chocolate with 1.5 oz. of butter, pour over the cake with chocolate icing. Let it harden for half an hour and remove the form from the finished cake.

RECIPE TIP
The recipe for this legendary Soviet cake was born in the confectionery workshop of the Praga restaurant, which was headed by Vladimir Guralnik.

QUICHE LORRAINE WITH SPINACH

Prep Time: 50 minutes

Servings: 6

INGREDIENTS
- Ham 8.8 oz.
- Spinach 7.1 oz.
- Comté cheese 3.5 oz.
- Carrot 1
- Milk 100 ml

- Sour cream 35% 7.1 oz.
- Nutmeg pinch
- Wheat flour 8.1 oz.
- Chicken eggs 4
- Butter 4.4 oz.
- Egg yolk 1
- Water 2 tablespoons
- Salt to taste
- Ground black pepper to taste

COOKING INSTRUCTIONS

1. Cut the ham and carrots into medium cubes. Wash and chop the spinach. Grate the cheese on a coarse grater.
2. In a hot skillet, lightly fry the ham, add the chopped carrots and continue to fry over medium heat until the carrots are ready. Add spinach, remove from heat, and close the lid.
3. Sift flour, butter, and salt together and mix with your hands until crumbs are present. Add egg yolk, mix, gradually pour in cold water (about two tablespoons), and knead thoroughly. Roll out the dough, shift into a form with sides.
4. In a bowl, mix half the grated cheese, sour cream, milk, eggs, and seasoning. Mix well. Add the fried ham with carrots and spinach to the bowl, mix again, pour into the form with the prepared crust, sprinkle with the

remaining cheese, and bake at a temperature of 350 degrees F for 30 minutes.

RECIPE TIP
Quiche Lorraine is one of the most frequently prepared pies in the world. Eggs, cheese, ham, nutmeg—all this is a classic. If you find the taste of classic Lorraine heavy, add more spinach.

KUTABY WITH HERBS

Prep Time: 15 minutes

Servings: 4

INGREDIENTS
- Fresh cilantro 1 bunch
- Wheat flour 2 cups
- Water ½ cup
- Butter 5.3 oz.
- Parsley 1 bunch
- Chives 1 bunch
- Salt 0.4 oz.

COOKING INSTRUCTIONS

1. Mix flour with salt, add a quarter cup of warm water, and mix. Pour in the remaining water, stirring constantly. Knead the cool dough.
2. Grind the herbs and mix with 3.5 oz. of melted butter.
3. Divide the dough into four equal parts, each of which is rolled into a thin pancake about 1 millimeter thick.
4. Put the filling in half of the rolled dough, cover with the second half and seal the edges with a fork. It is important that as little air as possible is left inside.
5. Put kutaby in a heated dry frying pan, fry for 2-3 minutes on each side over low heat. Grease finished kutaby with butter.

SACHER TORTE

Prep. Time: 30 minutes

Servings: 4

INGREDIENTS
- Egg yolks 7
- Butter 5.3 oz.
- Powdered sugar 4.4 oz.
- Dark chocolate 14.1 oz.
- Vanilla sugar 0.3 oz.
- Egg whites 7
- Sugar 13.2 oz.

- Salt just a pinch
- Wheat flour 5.3 oz.
- Apricot jam 7.1 oz.
- Water 170 ml

COOKING INSTRUCTIONS

1. Melt 7.1 oz. of chocolate in a water bath (the bowl should not touch the water).
2. Meanwhile, whisk the softened butter with icing sugar and vanilla sugar in a mixer. Gradually introduce the yolks.
3. Preheat the oven to 350 degrees F. Grease the cake pan. Beat the whites with a pinch of salt and 4.4 oz. of sugar until solid peaks form.
4. Add melted chocolate to the yolk mass. In turn, add the same egg whites and flour, trying not to disturb the egg whites for too long otherwise the cake will not be airy. Transfer the mass to a baking dish and bake for 1 hour.
5. Prepare apricot jam. If there are particles in it, it should be strained through a sieve or put in a blender until achieving a uniform consistency.
6. Remove the cake from the oven and allow to cool.
7. Cut the cake lengthwise into two parts. Cover the bottom with a generous layer of jam. Cover with the other half and spread jam on the cake on all sides.

8. To prepare the icing, break 200 g of chocolate into small pieces. Mix 250 g of sugar with 170 ml of water in a saucepan, heat for several minutes and allow to cool. Melt the chocolate in warm caramel.

9. Quickly cover the cake with icing (it is more convenient to put it on a baking rack installed on a baking sheet). Smooth the icing with a spatula and leave to harden at room temperature.

RECIPE TIP
The cake should not be stored in the refrigerator, as it will become condensed and lose its appearance.

FAST TIRAMISU WITH RASPBERRIES AND MINT

Prep Time: 15 minutes
Servings: 6

INGREDIENTS
- Mascarpone cheese 17.6 oz.
- Guinea fowl eggs 5
- Vanilla sugar 1.1 oz.
- Powdered sugar 3.5 oz.
- Ground coffee 4 tablespoons
- Cinnamon sticks 2
- Savoiardi cookies (Ladyfingers) 18

- Cocoa powder 0.4 oz.
- Disaronno amaretto liqueur 60 ml
- Raspberries 8.8 oz.
- Mint 6 stems

COOKING INSTRUCTIONS

1. Separate the egg whites from the yolks. They need to be whipped at an average speed of the mixer for about three minutes, and add the icing sugar to the yolks and beat too. Both should have a rather dense consistency.
2. Put the mascarpone in a bowl, pour in vanilla sugar and mix well. Gently introduce egg yolks and proteins into the cheese mass. Whisk everything again by hand, making sure that the mixture is homogeneous.
3. Pour boiling water over ground coffee and cinnamon sticks. While coffee is brewing (and it must be strong), break the Savoiardi cookies into halves and distribute them into six small bowls.
4. Pour 10 ml of Disaronno amaretto and 40-50 ml of coffee into each serving of cookies, add a mixture of mascarpone and beaten eggs to the bowls. Tiramisu can be refrigerated for a couple of hours or eaten immediately.
5. Sprinkle the finished dessert with cocoa using a strainer so that there are no lumps. Distribute a dozen raspberries in the center among the bowls of tiramisu, garnish with sprigs of mint, and serve.

CHOCOLATE FONDANT WITH ICE CREAM

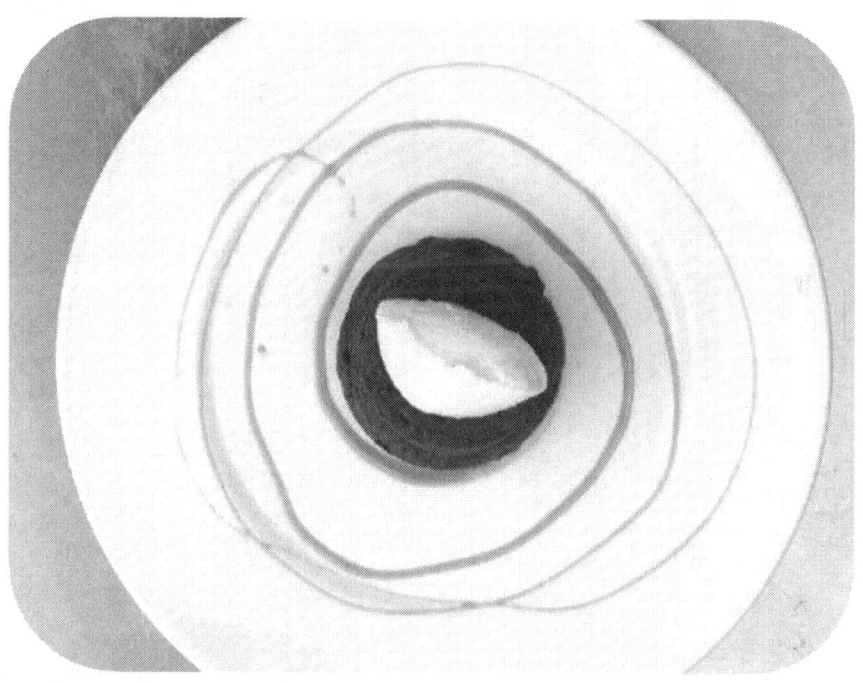

Prep Time: 45 minutes
Servings: 8

INGREDIENTS
- Butter 8.8 oz.
- Cocoa powder to taste
- Dark chocolate 7.1 oz.
- Brown sugar 7.1 oz.
- Caramel sauce to taste
- Ice cream 17.6 oz.

- Chicken eggs 4
- Egg yolks 4
- Wheat flour 7.1 oz.

COOKING INSTRUCTIONS

1. Melt 1.8 oz. butter. Grease the baking dishes (these ceramic molds are called ramekins) and refrigerate. When the butter hardens, coat with another layer.

2. Pour a teaspoon of cocoa into the mold. Slightly tilting the mold toward you, rotate it so that the cocoa completely covers the inside of the mold. Pour out excess powder.

3. In a water bath, melt the chocolate (having previously sorted it into segments) and the remaining butter. Remove the container from the fire, mix thoroughly until smooth, and let cool for about 10 minutes.

4. Beat eggs, yolks, and sugar in a bowl until a pale yellow mass forms. Sift the flour into the egg mixture and beat again. Gradually pour melted chocolate into the egg mixture, mix well.

5. Pour the dough onto the ramekins, allow to cool for twenty minutes. If necessary, the fondants can be frozen to cook later.

6. Preheat the oven to 430 degrees F. Put the fondants on a baking sheet, bake for 10 to 12 minutes until a crust

forms and the fondant itself begins to pull away slightly from the sides. If the fondant was frozen, leave it in the oven for 5 minutes longer. Take it out and let stand for one minute. You can slightly twist them in the ramekins so that they pull away from the sides. To make sure the fondant is not stuck, gently turn the ramekin over, covering it with the palm of your hand, then return it to its place before serving. To serve, garnish a plate with caramel sauce, place a fondant in the center, and lay a scoop of ice cream on top.

VANILLA CREME BRULEE

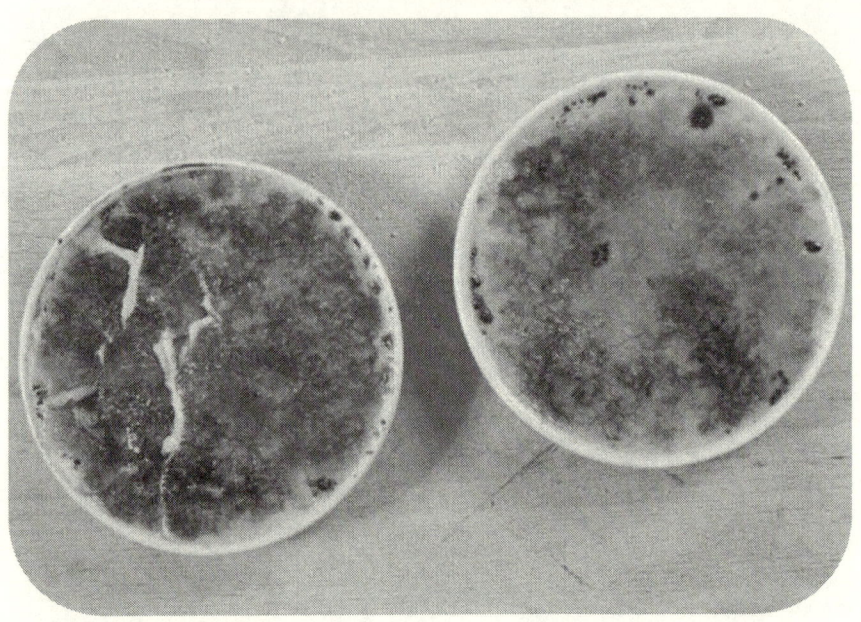

Prep Time: 50 minutes

Servings: 6

INGREDIENTS
- Chicken eggs 9
- Cream 33% 700 ml
- Vanilla pod 1
- Salt 0.05 oz.
- Sugar 6.4 oz.

COOKING INSTRUCTIONS

1. To the 9 egg yolks, add 180 grams of sugar and beat with a whisk. The mixture will change color from bright yellow to sandy white. When whipping, it is imperative to capture the edges of the mass. Under the influence of sugar, the yolks will begin to slowly "fry." If they are not removed, the taste of crème brûlée will be wrong.

2. Cut along the vanilla pod. Scrape the dark flesh from its half with a knife and mix thoroughly with whipped yolks. Combine the mixture with cold cream and salt. Strain through a fine sieve. This must be done so that pieces of yolk hardened by sugar do not get into the crème brûlée.

3. Arrange the molds for the crème brûlée in a deep heat-resistant tray and pour water so that portioned cups drown in it at two-thirds deep. Then pour the egg-cream mixture into the forms, filling them to the very edges. Put the pan in the oven, heated to 210 degrees F for 40 minutes.

4. The top of the finished crème brûlée should be elastic and inside the mass will remain liquid. Put the dishes in the refrigerator for a couple of hours to thicken the cream. To obtain a caramel crust, sprinkle the molds with an even layer of sugar and, melting it with a burner, turn the surface of the cream into a dark brown caramel lid.

5. Leave the crème brûlée alone for a short while. After a minute or two, the caramel will harden and the dessert will be ready. Now you can take a spoon and, as in *Amélie*, break the caramel crust and scoop up the cream with small black vanilla grains.

RECIPE TIP
The traditional crème brûlée has a vanilla flavor, but you can replace vanilla with lemon or orange peel, experiment with aromas of instant coffee, violets, rum, etc.

MERINGUE WITH CARDAMOM

Prep Time: 1 hour 20 minutes

Servings: 4

INGREDIENTS
- Sugar 1 cup
- Egg whites 3
- Ground cardamom 3/4 teaspoon

COOKING INSTRUCTIONS

1. In a large bowl, beat the chilled egg whites into a strong foam. Then gradually, whisking, add sugar, then cardamom.
2. Place in a pastry bag or spread them in a small pile on a baking sheet with a spoon.
3. Put in the oven 275 degrees F for 60-90 minutes until the meringues dry well. You can bring them to almost readiness, then turn off the oven and leave them to cool inside.

PLUM CRUMBLE

Prep Time: 30 minutes
Servings: 6

INGREDIENTS
- Wheat flour 7.1 oz.
- Butter 5.3 oz.
- Sugar 3.5 oz.
- Plums 35.3 oz.
- Oatmeal 7.1 oz.
- Cinnamon ½ teaspoon

COOKING INSTRUCTIONS

1. Mix cold butter with flour and sugar in a lumpy shortcrust pastry. Add oatmeal and mix. Put the dough on baking paper and bake in the oven, preheated to 340 F degrees, for 10 minutes.

2. Cut the plums in half, remove the pits, and put in a mold. Sprinkle with cinnamon, crumble the dough on top. Put in the oven, preheated to 340 degrees F, for 15 to 20 minutes.

BASBOUSA

Prep Time: 1 hour
Servings: 12

INGREDIENTS
- Semolina 14.8 oz.
- Coconut flakes 30.2 oz.
- Sugar 90.4 oz.
- Natural yogurt 7.1 oz.
- Vanilla extract 5 ml
- Wheat flour 2.7 oz.
- Butter 7.5 oz.
- Almond 1.1 oz.

- Water 250 ml
- Lemon juice 1 teaspoon

COOKING INSTRUCTIONS

1. Mix semolina, flour, 7.8 oz. sugar, coconut, yogurt, vanilla, and melted butter in a bowl. If the mixture seems too thick, you can add a little milk. Distribute the mixture in a greased pan.
2. Cut into diamonds and put almond in the center of each diamond. Bake in the oven, preheated to 370 degrees F, for 35-40 minutes until golden brown.
3. Prepare the syrup. In a saucepan, bring the water with sugar to a boil, stirring occasionally. Let it boil for 5 minutes without stirring, then add lemon juice and remove from heat.
4. Pour syrup over the hot cake and allow to cool. Serve cold.

STRAWBERRY PIE WITH CRÈME PATISSIER

Prep Time: 1 hour

Servings: 4

INGREDIENTS
- Wheat flour 6 oz.
- Sugar 7.9 oz.
- Baking powder 1 teaspoon
- Butter 4.4 oz.
- Chicken eggs 2
- Milk 300 ml

- Starch 0.7 oz.
- Vanilla pod 1
- Egg yolks 2
- Strawberries 17.6 oz.
- Salt to taste

COOKING INSTRUCTIONS

1. Pour 150 grams of flour, 100 grams of sugar, salt, and baking powder onto the work surface. In the middle of the hill, make a valley. Break one egg into it and beat with a fork. Add chilled butter in slices and knead the dough by hand.
2. Wrap the finished dough in a transparent film and leave it in the refrigerator for 30 minutes.
3. Beat the egg, yolks, and remaining sugar until white in a heat-resistant bowl. Sift 0.7 oz. of flour and starch, beat.
4. Bring milk and vanilla seeds to a boil, remove from heat. Pour into the egg mass in a thin stream, stirring constantly.
5. Put a bowl in a saucepan 1/3 filled with slightly boiling water and cook until thick, about 7 minutes, stirring constantly so that the eggs do not curdle.
6. Put the finished cream through a sieve and cool by covering the surface of the cream with a film, pressing it down so that it completely fits.

7. Distribute the dough in the mold. The thickness of the cake should be about five millimeters. Bake in a preheated oven to 320 degrees F for 40 minutes.

8. Remove the finished cake from the mold and cool. Layer the cream over it, about 1 cm thick. Top with a thick hill of strawberries.

PUMPKIN PIE

Prep Time: 1 hour 30 minutes

Servings: 8

INGREDIENTS
- Pumpkin 35.3 oz.
- Filo dough 17.6 oz.
- Sugar 7.1 oz.
- Ground cinnamon to taste
- Walnuts 3.5 oz.
- Butter 7.1 oz.
- Egg yolk 1

COOKING INSTRUCTIONS
1. Peel and grate the pumpkin. Finely chop the nuts.
2. Line the filo sheet on the table and grease it with melted butter. Put another sheet of dough on top and grease it with butter too.
3. Pour a portion of grated pumpkin onto the dough, top with a few nuts, cinnamon, and sugar.
4. Twist the dough into a sausage, bending it on the sides so that the filling does not fall out.
5. Place the resulting sausage with a spiral in the center of a round shape, also previously greased with melted butter.
6. Repeat the procedure several times. Place each new sausage as a continuation of the previous one. The result should be one big spiral resembling a snail.
7. Grease the pie with a slightly broken yolk, sprinkle with sugar and cinnamon. Bake in the oven, preheated to 360 degrees F, for 30-40 minutes.

CHAPTER 4 «LUNCH RECIPES»

Have you ever craved a healthy mid-day meal at work? The first thing that comes to mind is to go to a nearby fast-food restaurant, such as Burger King or McDonald's, and buy a greasy burger, crispy French fries, and a Coca-Cola. Thinking of all the fast food you want to eat, especially with the short amount of time you have, you should instead consider planning a proper lunch. If you are conscious of your health, then you have to make your own lunch. The good news is, this is what I am here for. This section consists of some healthy, tasty, and simple lunch recipes.

The Importance of a Healthy Lunch

Lunch is an important meal of your day, so don't ignore it even if you prefer breakfast. Many people think that eating a big breakfast means that no lunch is needed, but this is not the case. When you do not eat lunch, you are more likely to eat unhealthy food during the day or overeat during dinner time. When you do not eat lunch, your body runs out of nutrients, so it is best to always have lunch, even if this means using an extra day of free time. No matter what your special needs are, there are ways to ensure that your lunch is healthy and flavorful.

If you work at a company or school during lunch time, you can save a lot of money by bringing lunch instead of buying it at a fast food restaurant or place. Your special diet will be more nutritious and in many cases tastier. If you are not an early riser, eating lunch does not mean that you must get up early to prepare. Just pack it the night before. Numerous recipe options can help you prepare a lunch that your colleagues will envy.

You may also consider stopping at the supermarket for frozen diet meals. These meal options are usually low in fat and nutritious, and there are enough types to eat different lunches every week. Sometimes this option may be more expensive than preparing your own lunch, but it might be a little cheaper. Remember to look at the packaging to determine the best frozen meals. Some meals are not suitable for those of us who want a healthy diet. Although they may taste good, they are full of preservatives and calories.

Nutritious Lunch

Food is what gives you energy. In a world where everything is getting faster by the minute, people usually forget lunch. But the fact is lunch is not a waste of time. It is essential to the body and makes you more productive, not to mention the refreshment it provides. Lunch causes a surge of energy in the body and helps you to focus for the remainder of the afternoon. It a fact that those who don't eat lunch tend to gain extra weight because they overeat when it comes to dinner in order to compensate for the meal they missed. There are several other important reasons for eating a healthy nutritious lunch. While they are too numerous to mention, I am sure you know some of them, which is why you bought this book. Consider the tasty and simple lunch recipes in this chapter and let me know what you think.

CREAMY KOHLRABI SPIRALS WITH CHICKEN BREAST

Prep Time: 30 to 60 minutes

Servings: 4

INGREDIENTS

For the chicken breast:
- 2 chicken breasts (with skin, free-range chicken)
- 1 tablespoon of olive oil
- 1 branch of rosemary

- salt
- pepper

For the béchamel sauce:
- 0.9 oz. butter
- 2 shallots (peeled, finely chopped)
- 0.9 oz. of flour
- 250 ml milk
- salt
- pepper (from the mill)
- nutmeg

For the vegetables:
- 2 kohlrabi (peeled)
- 7.1 oz. peas
- 4 carrots (mini)
- pea sprouts (for garnish)

COOKING INSTRUCTIONS

1. For the creamy kohlrabi spirals with chicken breast, first put rosemary under the skin of the chicken breast. Fry the chicken breast in a hot pan on the skin side. Season with salt and pepper, turn over and put in the oven at 320 degrees F for 8-10 minutes. Take the chicken breast out of the pan and cut into elongated slices.
2. For the béchamel sauce, sweat the shallots in a saucepan with butter, stir in the flour, and briefly fry. Pour in milk

and cook with constant stirring. Season with salt, pepper, and nutmeg.

3. Remove the shell from the peas. Peel the mini carrots. Blanch both briefly in salt water.
4. Cut kohlrabi with a spiral cutter and blanch briefly in salted water. Warm up briefly in the béchamel sauce with half of the young peas.
5. Arrange kohlrabi spirals on a plate, sprinkle with peas, place mini carrots and chicken strips on top and finish with pea sprouts. Serve creamy kohlrabi spirals with chicken breast.

TIP
This dish may also be served with fresh herbs.

ZUCCHINI MEATBALLS WITH MOZZARELLA

Prep Time: 30 to 60 minutes

Servings: 4

INGREDIENTS
- 17.6 oz. minced meat (mixed)
- 1 onion
- 2 cloves of garlic
- 2 eggs
- 1 pinch of salt

- ➢ 1 pinch of pepper (colored)
- ➢ 1 pack of mozzarella (mini)
- ➢ 2.1 oz. breadcrumbs
- ➢ 1/2 zucchini
- ➢ 3 tbsp rapeseed oil

COOKING INSTRUCTIONS

1. For the zucchini meatballs with mozzarella, put the minced meat in an appropriately sized bowl. Finely chop the onion and the garlic; finely grate the zucchini with a kitchen grater.
2. Add all of this to the minced meat. Break the eggs and add with the breadcrumbs. Season with salt and pepper, then knead until everything is well-mixed. Flatten a little of the meat mass in your hand, place a small mozzarella ball in the center, close the meat mass tightly around it, and shape it into a ball. Roll it in breadcrumbs.
3. Heat the oil to 360 degrees F in a saucepan and fry the meatballs until crispy for a few minutes.
4. (As a healthier variant, you can also prepare the meatballs in the oven. To do this, preheat the oven with circulating air to 360 degrees F. Then place the balls on a baking tray lined with baking paper and bake on a medium rack for about 20-25 minutes until they are done.)

5. Seasonal vegetables and potatoes are recommended as an accompaniment to the zucchini meatballs with mozzarella.

TIP
These zucchini meatballs also taste very good when cooked with feta. Here you would need less salt because feta cheese itself is very salty.

The meatballs are also wonderful as finger food for parties.

PASTA WITH CHARD AND BACON

Prep Time: 15 to 30 minutes
Servings: 4

INGREDIENTS
- 14.1 oz. pasta (e.g. ribbon pasta)
- 4 chard leaves
- 21.2 oz. strips of bacon
- 4 sticks green onion
- 2 shallots
- 150 ml Grüner Veltliner wine

- 1 tbsp butter (large)
- mint (as a garnish)
- 1 tbsp sunflower oil
- 1.8 oz. white bread
- 5 tbsp herbs (roughly chopped, e.g. mint, chervil, parsley, chives)
- salt
- pepper

COOKING INSTRUCTIONS

1. For the pasta with Swiss chard and bacon, boil the pasta al dente in plenty of salted water, drain, and set aside about 100 ml of the cooking water.
2. Cut the chard and the green onion into thick pieces; peel the shallot and finely dice.
3. Mix the white bread finely with the herbs.
4. Fry the bacon until crispy in a pan with a tablespoon of sunflower oil, remove from the pan. Fry the chard, shallots, and green onions in the remaining oil.
5. Deglaze with the white wine, add the pasta water and the butter, and bring to a boil once. Then mix in the pasta and the herb crumbs, and season with salt and pepper. Garnish the pasta with fresh mint before serving.

TIP
When Swiss chard is not in season, just use fresh spinach or arugula.

POTATO PANCAKES FILLED WITH CHEESE

Prep Time: 15 to 30 minutes

Servings: 2

INGREDIENTS

- 21.2 oz. potatoes (floury)
- 1 onion (small)
- 1 egg
- 1 tbsp potato starch (up to 2 tbsp)

- 2.8 oz. mountain cheese
- 2 tbsp white wine vinegar
- 4 tablespoons of olive oil
- 1 tsp mustard (spicy)
- 1 oak leaf lettuce
- pepper
- nutmeg
- salt
- clarified butter

COOKING INSTRUCTIONS

1. For the potato pancakes filled with cheese, peel the potatoes and grate them finely. Put them in a kitchen towel and squeeze well so that a dry potato mass is formed.

2. Chop or grate the onion and add it together with the egg to the amount of potatoes, season with nutmeg and salt. Bake a small sample buffer in a frying pan with clarified butter. If necessary, add a little bit of potato starch to the amount.

3. Cut the cheese into thumb-length, 2 cm wide pieces and cover with the amount of potatoes. Bake the potato and cheese pancakes in a frying pan with clarified butter.

4. Stir vinegar, oil, and mustard well and season with salt and freshly ground pepper. Drizzle this dressing over the cleaned lettuce and serve it with the potato pancakes filled with cheese.

TIP

A sour cream dip with herbs also tastes great with these cheese-filled potato pancakes.

ASIAN CHICKEN WINGS WITH STRAWBERRY AND MELON SALAD

Prep Time: 30 to 60 minutes

Servings: 4

INGREDIENTS

For the Asian chicken wings:
- 35.3 oz. chicken wings
- 3 tbsp soy sauce
- 2 tbsp honey

- 1 tsp cilantro seeds
- 1/2 tsp chili (ground)
- 1 piece of ginger (small)
- 2 tbsp cornstarch

For the salad:
- 8.8 oz. strawberries
- 5.3 oz. melon
- 1.8 oz. arugula
- 50 ml balsamic vinegar
- 50 ml olive oil
- 1 tsp pepper (pink)
- salt

COOKING INSTRUCTIONS

1. For chicken wings with strawberry melon salad, peel the ginger and grate finely. Pound cilantro with a mortar. Mix with soy sauce, honey, chili, and ginger. Marinate the chicken wings with it (approx. 20 minutes) and rub the cornstarch in. Then cook on a grill or in a preheated oven at approx. 360 degrees F until crispy.

2. Wash the strawberries, remove the green tops, and cut them into bite-size pieces. Peel the melon, core if necessary, and cut into thin strips with a peeler. Wash the arugula, drain, and mix with the remaining ingredients. Let it steep for about 5 minutes.

3. Serve the chicken wings with strawberry and melon salad.

TIP
For this recipe, you can choose melons to suit your own taste. If you want it even more fruity, use a little mint instead of arugula.

TATAR AZU

Prep Time: 30 minutes

Servings: 4

INGREDIENTS
- Beef 17.6 oz.
- Bulb onions 5 heads
- Salted cucumbers 3
- Tomato paste 2 tablespoons
- Potatoes 1 kg
- Meat broth 1 cup
- Garlic 3 cloves
- Bay leaves 2

COOKING INSTRUCTIONS

1. Rinse the meat, cut into strips, and lightly fry in a cauldron in warmed vegetable oil.
2. Add chopped onion into thin rings and fry the meat with onion until the onion is soft.
3. Add tomato paste, finely chopped or grated cucumbers on a coarse grater. Pour in water or broth and simmer under the lid until the meat is fully cooked.
4. Fry the chopped potatoes in a separate pan.
5. When the potato is almost ready, transfer it to the cauldron with stew, add salt, pepper, bay leaf, and minced or finely chopped garlic.
6. Gently mix and simmer the potatoes with meat until cooked for about 5-7 minutes.

RATATOUILLE

Prep Time: 25 minutes

Servings: 4

INGREDIENTS
- Eggplants 2
- Yellow bell pepper 1
- Red bell pepper 1
- Bulb onion 1 head
- Garlic 2 cloves
- Tomatoes 2
- Sugar pinch

- Olive oil 50 ml
- Tomato paste ½ teaspoon
- Parsley 0.4 oz.
- Salt to taste
- Ground black pepper to taste

COOKING INSTRUCTIONS

1. Cut the onion and eggplant into small cubes. Sprinkle the eggplant with salt and let it rest for several minutes to let the juice flow.
2. Peel the peppers and tomatoes, and cut the flesh in the same small cubes as the eggplant and onions. Finely chop the garlic and parsley.
3. Heat part of the olive oil in a frying pan, fry the onions until soft, and put them in a colander.
4. Add a little oil to the pan, fry the eggplant cubes (previously drained of excess liquid) until soft. Place the fried eggplant in a colander. Fry the cubes of bell pepper in the same oil and also throw them into the colander.
5. Pour the remaining oil into the pan, fry the garlic until soft, immediately add the tomato paste and a pinch of sugar, and then immediately the tomatoes. Stew for thirty seconds, then mix in all the previously fried vegetables and chopped parsley, salt, pepper, and darken for a minute before removing from heat.

IDAHO POTATOES

Prep Time: 1 hour
Servings: 3

INGREDIENTS
- New potatoes 10
- Extra virgin olive oil 250 ml
- Dill 1 bunch
- Parsley 1 bunch
- Garlic 3 cloves

- Red Tabasco sauce 1 teaspoon
- Salt to taste

COOKING INSTRUCTIONS

1. Rinse the potatoes well (do not peel). Cut lengthwise into eight slices, put in a pan with cold salted water.
2. Bring to a boil and cook for 2-3 minutes. Drain and let the potatoes cool.
3. Mix olive oil with finely chopped herbs, sauce, and garlic squeezed through a garlic crusher. Put the potatoes on a baking sheet in one layer, after dipping the slices in the resulting mixture.
4. Bake in the oven for 15–20 minutes at a temperature of 390 degrees F.

RECIPE TIP
I recommend using a non-stick baking sheet or, if using a regular baking sheet, place parchment paper under the potatoes.

GRATIN DAUPHINOIS

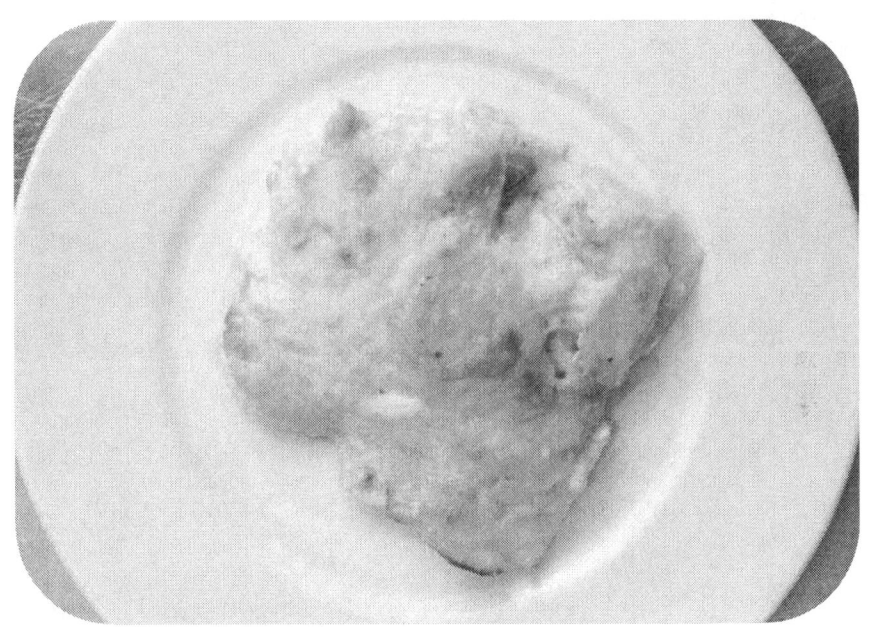

Prep Time: 1 hour 5 minutes

Servings: 4

INGREDIENTS
- Potatoes 21.2 oz.
- Milk 300 ml
- Cream 48% 100 ml
- Nutmeg ½ teaspoon
- Gruyere cheese 3.5 oz.
- Garlic 4 cloves
- Salt to taste
- Ground black pepper to taste

COOKING INSTRUCTIONS

1. Peel the potatoes and cut them into thin slices (2-3 mm), most conveniently on a mandoline. When thinly cutting the potatoes, do not wash them so as not to splash the starch with water, which will be needed to thicken the cream.

2. In a saucepan over medium heat, bring milk and cream to a boil. Add potatoes and mix so that the potatoes are covered with a layer of cream. Season with nutmeg, salt, and pepper.

3. Reduce the heat and cook for 8 to 10 minutes, stirring so that the mixture does not stick to the bottom of the pan. After the potatoes are ready, mix the grated cheese into the milk, potatoes, and cream, and then remove the pan from the heat.

4. Crush the garlic and mix it with the potatoes and everything else. The mixture is poured into a deep pan and baked in an oven, preheated to 250 degrees F, for 25 minutes.

5. The gratin is ready when the tip of a sharp knife easily pierces it (at the same time, the knife should not go into the oil, you should still feel some resistance). To make the casserole brown, put it on the very top shelf in the oven and turn on the maximum heat for about a minute. Before serving, allow the potatoes to cool slightly to slightly thicken the creamy cheese sauce.

CARROT CUTLETS

Prep Time: 30 minutes
Servings: 4

INGREDIENTS
- Carrots 1 kg
- Milk ½ cup
- Semolina ½ cup
- Breadcrumbs ½ cup
- Chicken eggs 3
- Sugar 1 teaspoon
- Vegetable oil 3 tablespoons

COOKING INSTRUCTIONS

1. Thinly peel washed carrots into slices or straws. Put in a saucepan, pour hot milk over them, add a tablespoon of butter, sugar, and salt. Cover and simmer until cooked over medium heat, stirring so that the carrots do not burn.
2. When the carrots are ready, sprinkle them with semolina and, stirring, cook over low heat for 8-10 minutes.
3. Remove the carrots from the heat, put in the egg yolks, mix well, and cool.
4. From the chilled mass, cook the cutlets moistened with egg white, roll in breadcrumbs, and fry on both sides. Serve with sour cream or milk sauce.

COD WITH TOMATOES

Prep Time: 15 minutes

Servings: 6

INGREDIENTS
- Cod fillet 1.2 kg
- Olive oil 6 tablespoons
- Lemons 2
- Parsley 4.2 oz.
- Cherry tomatoes 24
- Salt to taste
- Ground black pepper to taste

COOKING INSTRUCTIONS

1. In six heat-resistant bags for cooking in the oven, put in a piece of cod, a tablespoon of chopped parsley, four tomatoes cut in half, one quarter lemon juice, and a tablespoon of oil.
2. Salt and pepper the contents, tie the bags securely, and bake in the oven for 15 minutes, heated to 360 degrees F.

RECIPE TIP

Usually, salted cod is used for this dish, which is pre-soaked for a long time in fresh water. This dish can be served with mashed potatoes or boiled potatoes. You should not season the potatoes or mashed potatoes with anything. The cod sauce is enough to add flavor.

SHRIMP AND CHICKEN PAELLA

Prep Time: 40 minutes

Servings: 4

INGREDIENTS
- Round rice 10.6 oz.
- Garlic 4 cloves
- Bulb onion 1 head
- Bell pepper 1
- Green peas 3.5 oz.

- Shrimp 7.1 oz.
- Chicken thighs 17.6 oz.
- Chicken bouillon 1 liter
- Black peppercorns 4
- Tomatoes 2
- Lemon 2
- Saffron pinch
- Olive oil 100 ml
- Parsley 1.8 oz.
- Salt to taste
- Ground black pepper to taste
- Dry white wine 200 ml

COOKING INSTRUCTIONS

1. Chop the chicken thighs into smaller pieces and fry in a deep pan in olive oil until half ready.
2. Finely chop the onion and fry with the chicken. When the onions become soft, add finely chopped garlic and rice. Fry it all for two to three minutes. Then pour finely chopped peppers and tomatoes into the pan. Stir and simmer for another minute or two, stirring so that the contents of the pan do not burn.
3. Heat the chicken stock and dilute a pinch of saffron in it. Pour it over the rice with vegetables and chicken, add salt, pepper, toss in a few black peppercorns, and cook for

ten minutes over low heat. If the broth reduces more than you planned, add more chicken broth, water, or dry white wine.

4. Next, add the peas to the rice and mix. Put the shrimp on top, pour the lemon juice, sprinkle with chopped parsley, and bring the paella to cook over three to four minutes over the same low heat, cover with a lid.

5. Serve with pink Catalan or Valencia wine. Very cold.

RECIPE TIP
Paella is primarily a deep frying pan, rice, and saffron. Everything else is optional. But if the rest appears, then often it's a whimsical combinations of vegetables, meat, and seafood. Paella got its name from the pan of the same name. At the same time, paella is always prepared with rice and almost always with saffron, but not necessarily in a special paella pan. It can also turn out very well in pans not specially designed for paella.

HAKE IN GREEN GARLIC SAUCE

Prep Time: 30 minutes

Servings: 2

INGREDIENTS
- Hake 4 pieces
- Garlic 3 cloves
- Minced parsley 3 tablespoons
- Fresh bay leaf 1
- Extra virgin olive oil 4 tablespoons

COOKING INSTRUCTION

1. Peel the garlic cloves and chop finely. Chop the leaves of parsley thoroughly (from half of a moderate bunch, you should get three full tablespoons of greens).

2. Heat four tablespoons of olive oil in a frying pan over medium heat. Once the oil is warm, add the garlic, and then the whole parsley after a couple of minutes.

3. Dry the hake steaks with paper towels, lightly salt, and put in a pan so that they do not touch each other. Add the bay leaf.

4. Fry the fish for 10 to 12 minutes, then gently turn over with a flat and thin spatula, holding the fish with your hands, and fry the other side for the same amount.

5. Put the prepared steaks on plates, top with green garlic sauce, and serve right away. They're best accompanied by young boiled potatoes.

RECIPE TIP

The temperature of the oil in the pan should be such that the garlic and parsley will fry for a very long time without burning, but not quite stewed. Hake turns out to be very tender, not the same as I remember in Soviet times.

BURGUNDY BEEF

Prep Time: 3 hours

Servings: 4

INGREDIENTS
- Beef 35.3 oz.
- Dry red wine 1 liter
- Garlic 4 cloves
- Bulb onion 1 head
- Parsley 0.7 oz.
- Thyme 2 stems
- Bay leaf 1
- Black peppercorns 8

- Bacon 3.5 oz.
- Butter 1.8 oz.
- Olive oil 50 ml
- Wheat flour 2 tablespoons
- Vegetable oil 50 ml
- Carrots 4
- Shallots 12
- Mushrooms 17.6 oz.
- Salt to taste
- Ground black pepper to taste

COOKING INSTRUCTIONS

1. Cut beef into large cubes, cut onions into half rings, and crush the garlic with the flat side of a knife. Put meat, onions, garlic, parsley, bay leaves, thyme, and black peppercorns in a deep bowl and pour in the red wine. Stir and refrigerate for 24 hours. Take the meat out of the finished marinade, dry the pieces on a napkin. Cut the bacon into small cubes and fry in a pan in vegetable oil until golden brown.

2. Remove the bacon from the pan and fry the beef in fat and oil until a brown crust forms. Add flour, mix, and fry for another minute.

3. Extract the meat and transfer it to a deep saucepan. Strain the marinade through a sieve and add it to the

meat. Pour fried bacon into the saucepan and let the meat stew.

4. After about an hour and a half, heat the pan and fry coarsely chopped carrots in a mixture of olive oil and butter until golden brown. Pour the carrots into the meat, simmer another 20 minutes.

5. Fry peeled shallots with whole small onions in the same pan. Sprinkle the onions in a saucepan and simmer for another 20 minutes.

6. Cut the mushrooms into halves and fry them in the same pan. Add to the skillet the meat and onions. Add the broth, salt, and pepper. Simmer for another 20 to 25 minutes. Remove from heat and serve with mashed potatoes or rice.

RECIPE TIP
This is the main meat dish of French gastronomy from the twentieth century. There are a million recipes, this one is the simplest. If the sauce is not thick enough, you can thicken it with corn starch after diluting it with a little warm water.

CHICKEN PICASSO

Prep Time: 45 minutes

Servings: 4

INGREDIENTS
- Chicken breasts 4
- Onions 2
- Bell peppers 3
- Garlic 3 cloves
- Tomatoes 4
- Vegetable bouillon cube 1
- Cheese 3.5 oz.

- ➤ Mix of Italian herbs 1 tablespoon
- ➤ Water ½ cup
- ➤ Cream ½ cup
- ➤ Olive oil 2 tablespoons
- ➤ Nutmeg pinch
- ➤ Salt to taste
- ➤ Butter 1 tablespoon
- ➤ Ground black pepper to taste

COOKING INSTRUCTIONS

1. Cut the bell pepper into rings (it is better to choose three different colors, it looks more colorful) after removing the seeds. Cut the onion in half rings; grate the garlic on a fine grater.
2. Take the chicken breast, salt, and pepper. In a combination of 2 tablespoons of olive oil and 1 tablespoon of butter, fry the breasts until golden brown. Transfer to oven pan.
3. In the same pan, fry the onions until golden brown, then transfer to the chicken.
4. Lightly fry the bell pepper rings until they become soft; add to the chicken.
5. Place the grated garlic in a pan, sauté for 30 seconds, then add water. Add chopped tomatoes (the skin can be removed beforehand), mix well. Add Italian herbs,

vegetable bouillon cube, salt, pepper, a pinch of nutmeg. Pour in half a glass of cream and mix.

6. Boil the sauce for 5 minutes over low heat. Pour it over the chicken and vegetables. Cover with foil, place in the oven at 390 degrees F for 30 minutes.

7. Remove, sprinkle with grated cheese. Place the chicken back into the oven, but without foil, for another 15 minutes until the cheese melts.

BEEF STROGANOFF

Prep Time: 30 minutes

Servings: 6

INGREDIENTS

- White mushrooms 17.6 oz. Sour cream 30% 5.3 oz.
- Cream 35% 100 ml
- Beef tenderloin 35.3 oz.
- Beef broth 500 ml
- Dry white wine 100 ml
- Salt to taste
- Vegetable oil 100 ml
- Dijon mustard 1 tablespoon
- Ground black pepper to taste

COOKING INSTRUCTIONS
1. Cut the beef tenderloin into thin slices, 3-5 mm each.
2. Preheat the pan and fry the slices of meat in vegetable oil, having previously salted them. Cook only until a brown crust appears, then put it in a warm place. (It is not necessary to fry the meat all at once. It's best to cook it in parts so that the pieces are not stewed together.)
3. Pour white wine into a stewpan and evaporate it to three quarters over high heat. Add the broth, it should be boiled about halfway.
4. In a pan with vegetable oil, fry sliced white mushrooms till brown and remove from heat.
5. Add cream and sour cream to the stewpan with broth and simmer over medium heat, preventing the sauce from escaping over the edge. When the sauce thickens, season it with salt and pepper.
6. Put the fried meat in a pan with mushrooms. Pour the sauce over it, bring it to a boil, and simmer the meat for another three minutes.
7. Add Dijon mustard to the beef stroganoff. Mix and serve with rice or noodles.

RECIPE TIP
In the dining tradition it was considered a stew, but in general it was fried meat with sauce. This dish is much brighter.

KHINKALI

Prep Time: 45 minutes

Servings: 3

INGREDIENTS
- Wheat flour 17.6 oz.
- Water 300 ml
- Salt 1.5 teaspoons
- Veal 8.8 oz.
- Beef 8.8 oz.
- Fat 3.5 oz.
- Bulb onions 3.5 oz.
- Garlic 2 cloves

- Ground cumin to taste
- Red chili peppers to taste
- Cilantro to taste

COOKING INSTRUCTIONS

1. Meat free of veins, such as brisket or tenderloin, is ground into minced meat. Add lard, finely chopped onions, and garlic. Add water—as much as the minced meat can absorb without being divided. About a pound of meat to about 150 ml. To taste, you can add salt, cumin, hot pepper (you can cook yourself), and cilantro.

2. Knead the dough from flour, salt, and 150 ml of water so it is sufficiently dense and tight. It will be difficult to knead and roll it manually; therefore, if you have a dough mixer and especially a dough sheeter, the process would be greatly facilitated. The dough can be stored in a cool place for no more than an hour, then it begins to rapidly lose its qualities.

3. The success of future khinkali depends on the number of layers in the test: ideally, there should be about twenty of them. To do this, roll out the dough with a rolling pin in a centimeter layer and cut it into 4 x 4 cm squares. Each piece must be rolled out and folded, sprinkled with flour every time, again and again—at least 10 times. The result should be 3 mm thick puff sheets.

4. Stuffing is prepared in advance, because as soon as the sheets of dough are ready, you need to wrap the meat in them immediately so that the dough does not dry. In the middle of each sheet, put a small ladle of minced meat, about 40 grams. If the minced water has managed to emerge from the meat, you need to mix it well again before spreading it on the dough.

5. The edges of the sheet are folded accordion-style, as densely as possible. In an ideal khinkali, there are nineteen folds. Take the fortified bag in one hand and twist the other in the same direction as the folds were made and tear off the excess dough—the khinkali will have a dense stump on top. Put the khinkali on the board so that it forms a flat bottom, which will then be convenient to bite.

6. With a spatula, stir the boiling water in a spacious pan to have it flow in a circular motion. Add salt and toss a dozen khinkali. Again make a whirlpool, stirring the pan. The point is that the khinkali should not squeeze or stick to each other or to the bottom. Cook until the khinkali floats belly-up. Add another two to three minutes, just about ten minutes total. Take them out carefully with a slotted spoon.

7. The khinkali are laid out on a dish. As a rule, a multiple of ten is boiled at a time; each subsequent portion is

prepared anew. The final gesture before the meal starts is to sprinkle still wet, smoking khinkali with freshly ground black pepper. This immediately releases the right aroma from them and they may be eaten immediately.

8. Khinkali is eaten with the hands—a fork will pierce the dough and the broth, the khinkali juice, will spill onto the plate. You need to take the tail with one hand and with the second hold the ribs. Bite the side on top and suck the broth. Then eat, biting the dough and meat in equal proportions so that a piece of meat is constantly resting in a boat of dough. The tails that remain will show the number of khinkali eaten by the end.

RECIPE TIP
The taste of khinkali is very dependent on the quality of the water in the minced meat. Therefore, it is best to use good mineral water.

CHICKEN LIVERS IN SOUR CREAM

Prep Time: 30 minutes

Servings: 4

INGREDIENTS

- Chicken livers 21.2 oz.
- Sour cream 20% 17.6 oz.
- Bulb onion 1 head
- Butter 0.7 oz.
- Salt to taste
- Ground black pepper to taste

COOKING INSTRUCTIONS

1. Rinse the liver. If you have time to soak them in milk for 20 minutes, they will be

   even more tender. If there is no time, then trim the veins. Cut into small pieces.
2. Fry finely chopped onions in butter until golden.
3. Add the liver. Fry for 5-7 minutes until the red color disappears. Add salt and pepper.
4. Pour sour cream and simmer over medium heat for 10 minutes.

RECIPE TIP
Garnish with mashed potatoes or rice. Bon appétit!

LAZY CABBAGE ROLLS WITH CHICKEN

Prep Time: 40 minutes

Servings: 4

INGREDIENTS
- Chicken bouillon 1 liter
- Garlic 6 cloves
- Lemongrass 1.2 oz.
- Red onion 3.5 oz.
- Bay leaves 2
- Turnip 7.1 oz.

- Ginger 1.8 oz.
- Rice 17.6 oz.
- Black peppercorns 6
- Chicken fillet 10.6 oz.
- Soy sauce 2 tablespoons
- Cilantro 1.8 oz.
- Cane sugar 2 teaspoons
- Vegetable oil 50 ml
- Sushi rice vinegar 50 ml
- White cabbage 35.3 oz.

COOKING INSTRUCTIONS

1. Cut the chicken into small pieces.
2. In a deep saucepan (and preferably in a large wok pan or cauldron), heat vegetable oil over high heat and fry the chicken fillet until golden brown.
3. As soon as the chicken is browned, add diced turnips, onions in half rings, and ginger (chopped into thin straws).
4. Stew for 5 minutes, then add chopped white cabbage flakes.
5. When the cabbage starts to juice, lower the heat. Add finely chopped garlic, bay leaves, pepper, soy sauce, lemongrass, sugar, and vinegar. Mix and stew for a

couple more minutes, then pour in rice. Mix again and simmer for another 3 minutes.

6. Pour the chicken broth into the pan (wok, cauldron) and simmer the stuffed cabbage until cooked. Depending on the type of rice, this is 15 to 20 minutes.

7. When the rice is cooked, mix the contents of the pan (wok, cauldron) with coarsely chopped cilantro, remove from heat, and let sit under the lid for about 5 minutes. Serve with sour cream or coconut cream. Or simply by itself.

RECIPE TIP
Normally meat and rice are used to stuff the cabbage. But in this recipe, they do not need to be wrapped in leaves, only chopped into the cabbage; hence, this "lazy" dish.

CHICKEN KIEV CUTLETS

Prep Time: 50 minutes

Servings: 6

INGREDIENTS
- Chicken fillets 6
- Panko breadcrumbs 3.5 oz.
- Garlic 4 cloves
- Chicken eggs 2
- Cream 33% 100 ml
- Butter 7.1 oz.

- Parsley 0.7 oz.
- Vegetable oil 1 liter
- Chives 0.7 oz.
- Tarragon 0.4 oz.
- Salt to taste
- Ground black pepper to taste

COOKING INSTRUCTIONS

1. Use a fork to mix the room temperature butter with chopped herbs, crushed garlic, and salt. Roll the butter into a thin sausage shape, wrap it in plastic, and put it in the freezer so that it hardens.
2. The chicken fillet should be beaten between two sheets of cling wrap to a thickness of about 3-5 mm. Salt and pepper on both sides.
3. Cut a piece 8-10 cm long from the sausage-shaped butter and wrap it in a fillet. Place the fillets in the refrigerator for 15 minutes.
4. Beat cream with eggs, soak cutlets in egg-cream mixture, and then roll out in breadcrumbs.
5. Heat vegetable oil to a boil and toss the cutlets into it. Fry until they turn brown, and then place in the oven for 5 minutes.
6. Serve with salad and mashed potatoes, sprinkle with breadcrumbs.

RECIPE TIP
This is the main hit of all Russian restaurants and institutions around the world. The classics can be slightly corrected by making a breading of Japanese panko crackers and butter for the filling according to the sauce method for Burgundy snails.

MASHED POTATOES

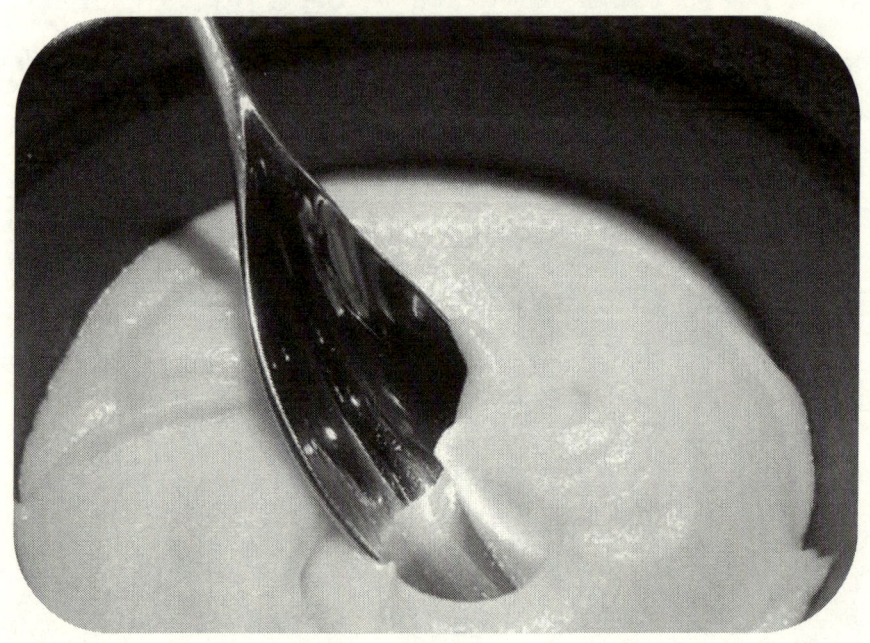

Prep Time: 50 minutes

Servings: 6

INGREDIENTS

- Potatoes 35.3 oz.
- Coarse salt 1 tablespoon
- Butter 8.8 oz.
- Fat milk 150 ml
- Salt to taste
- Ground black pepper to taste

COOKING INSTRUCTIONS

1. Rather than a starchy variety, Robuchon uses the French ratte variety of potato. Wash off the dirt without cutting off the skin. Put them in a pan, pour two liters of cold water over them, add a tablespoon of coarse salt, and bring it all to a light boil. Cook
for 25 minutes so that at the end a knife easily enters the clean potatoes.

2. Take out the potatoes, peel, and put them through a vegetable mill or potato press (although it's more labor-intensive, you can obtain the smoothest texture by putting them through a fine sieve).

3. Transfer the result to a pan, heat, and stir vigorously for five minutes.

4. Meanwhile, rinse a small frying pan under water, drain the remaining water, and pour milk into it without wiping it dry. Bring almost to a boil and keep hot.

5. Reduce the heat under the potatoes. Cut the butter (always cold) and add it to the potatoes piece by piece, vigorously mixing.

6. When the butter disappears, pour in the hot milk and, while mixing the potatoes forcefully, achieve the smoothness of the resulting mashed potatoes. Taste and season with salt and freshly ground black pepper.

RECIPE TIP

Robuchon's calling card is his mashed potatoes with their legendary texture and legendary amount of butter.

MINT-CRUSTED LAMB LEG

Prep Time: 1 hour 20 minutes

Servings: 4

INGREDIENTS
- Leg of lamb 1
- Fresh mint 7.1 oz.
- Sugar 2 tablespoons
- White wine vinegar 50 ml

- Olive oil 100 ml
- Balsamic vinegar 50 ml
- Ground black pepper 1 tablespoon
- Salt 1 teaspoon
- Thyme 3 stems

COOKING INSTRUCTIONS

1. Using the blender's pulse mode, turn a mixture of olive oil, mint, pepper, balsamic and white wine vinegar, sugar, salt, and thyme into a rough porridge. Allow the mint to retain some remnant of its form.
2. Thoroughly coat the lamb leg with this mixture, making sure to remove nearly all of the fat first. Leave in the mint marinade for two to three hours, wrapped in foil in the refrigerator.
3. Remove the leg from the refrigerator, put it on a baking sheet, and place in an oven preheated to 430 degrees F. Leave it at this temperature for 15 minutes. Then, reduce the heat to 360 degrees F and leave it for another 40 minutes. Turn the heat back up to 220 degrees and let it set in the oven for 10 more minutes. Remove from the oven, cut into thin slices, and serve with grilled vegetables.

BEEF DUMPLINGS

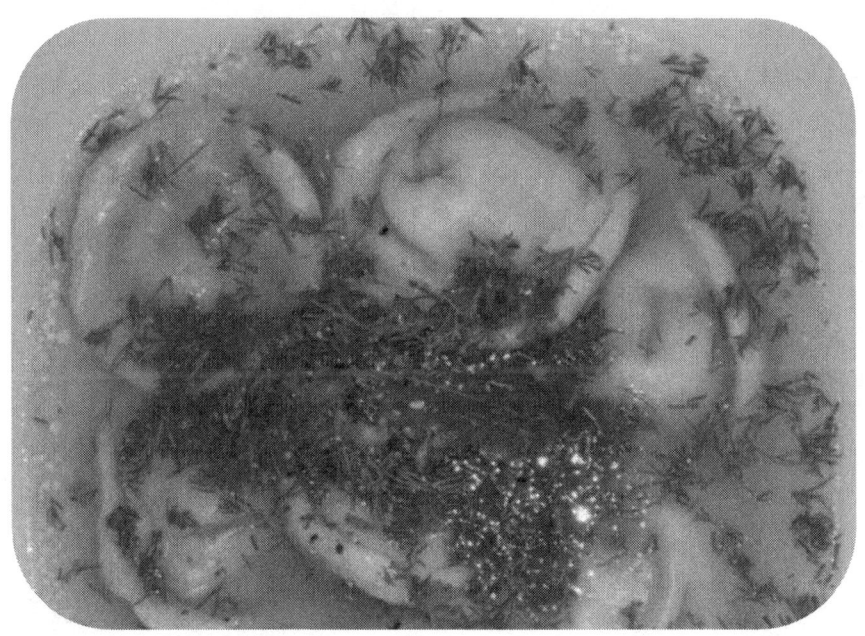

Prep Time: 30 minutes

Servings: 10

INGREDIENTS
- Dumpling dough 28.2 oz.
- Beef brisket 28.2 oz.
- Bulb onions 5.3 oz.
- Parsley 0.7 oz.
- Butter 2.5 oz.
- Dill 3 stems
- Bay leaves 3
- Black peppercorns 0.1 oz.

- Salt to taste
- Ground black pepper to taste

COOKING INSTRUCTIONS

1. For the minced meat, put the brisket (with not too much fat) and the butter through a meat grinder. Add finely chopped parsley and sautéed onions, salt and pepper to taste. Mix well and put in the refrigerator for exactly an hour to make the minced meat strong and elastic.

2. Roll out the dough with a rolling pin to a thickness of 1 mm and cut it into circles with a diameter of 4.5 cm. Put 5 grams of filling on each, fold in half, pinch the edges, and connect the corners.

3. Prepare the broth. Pour 5 liters of water into a pan with salt, bay leaves, black peppercorns, and whole dill. Toss dumplings into boiling water for 5-6 minutes until cooked.

BEEF WITH OYSTER SAUCE

Prep Time: 15 minutes

Servings: 4

INGREDIENTS
- Fresh cilantro 0.4 oz.
- Bulb onion ½ head
- Beef fillet 17.6 oz.
- Broccoli 14.1 oz.
- Ginger root 0.4 oz.

- Lemon ½
- Vegetable oil 50 ml
- Oyster sauce 50 ml

COOKING INSTRUCTIONS

1. Cut the beef fillet into thin slices. Finely chop the ginger and cut the onion into thin half rings. Disassemble broccoli into florets and boil for 3 minutes in water. Cool so that the florets do not lose their green color.
2. Heat the wok with vegetable oil and quickly fry the sliced meat to a bronze crust.
3. Add onion and ginger to the pan, and then the oyster sauce and broccoli after a minute. Fry for another minute or two, stirring constantly. Remove from heat and season with lemon juice and finely chopped cilantro.

RECIPE TIP

This dish can be served with fresh rice, as well as rice or egg noodles. They can be boiled and added directly to the wok before the lemon juice and cilantro, and mixed with the meat and vegetables.

CHICKEN WITH YOGURT, SESAME SEEDS, LEMON, AND GARLIC SAUCE

Prep Time: 20 minutes
Servings: 6

INGREDIENTS
- Potatoes 21.2 oz.
- Garlic 2 cloves
- Chicken drumsticks 18
- Lemon 1
- Sugar 1 tablespoon

- Soy sauce 50 ml
- Yogurt 300 ml
- White wine vinegar 20 ml
- Honey 1 tablespoon
- Butter 1.8 oz.
- Olive oil 100 ml
- Sesame oil 50 ml
- Sesame seeds 1.8 oz.
- Thyme 10 stems
- Parsley 0.7 oz.
- Salt to taste
- Ground black pepper to taste

COOKING INSTRUCTIONS

1. Remove excess fat from the chicken drumsticks, if any.
2. Pickle the chicken for half an hour in a mixture of soy sauce, honey, olive oil, thyme, sugar, vinegar, salt, and pepper.
3. Place in an oven, preheated to 360 degrees F, for 25 minutes.
4. Boil the potatoes and fry in butter.
5. Place sesame seeds, yogurt, parsley, lemon juice, two cloves of garlic, and sesame oil in a blender. Season with salt and pepper and turn into a green sauce. Serve chicken and potatoes with the sauce.

BAKED CHICKEN WITH VEGETABLES

Prep Time: 1 hour 20 minutes

Servings: 4

INGREDIENTS
- Chicken hen 45.8 oz.
- Red onion 1 head
- Yellow onion 1 head
- Garlic 4 cloves

- Parsley 0.7 oz.
- Carrot 1
- Butter 1.8 oz.
- Celery 1 stalk
- Bouquet garni 1
- Vegetable oil 50 ml

COOKING INSTRUCTIONS

1. Get rid of fat in the chicken's abdominal region and chest area. To extract fat from the breast, you need to make an incision on the skin of the back and turn the skin out, as if you were removing a sweater from the chicken. Then the skin should be pulled back on, covering the incision.
2. Chop red onion and garlic and fry in butter until soft. Do not overcook until golden. Stir fried onions and garlic with finely chopped parsley.
3. Stuff the chicken belly with this mixture, but not completely (only halfway, otherwise the chicken will not be fried). Put a slice of butter in the same place, and then tie the chicken legs with culinary thread. Chop off the tip from each wing and tie them tightly to the sides. These manipulations are necessary so that the chicken is juicy, while the meat remains elastic.
4. Fry the chicken on all sides in vegetable oil until golden brown.

5. Put the chicken on a baking sheet and fry coarsely chopped onions, carrots, and celery in a frying pan in the chicken's oil. Transfer vegetables to the same baking sheet, add a garnish bouquet, and place in the oven (350 degrees F) for 50 minutes.

RECIPE TIP
The readiness of the chicken can be determined by piercing it in the thigh area with a needle or knife. If the juice from the cut is clear, then the chicken is ready.

ROSEMARY CHICKEN

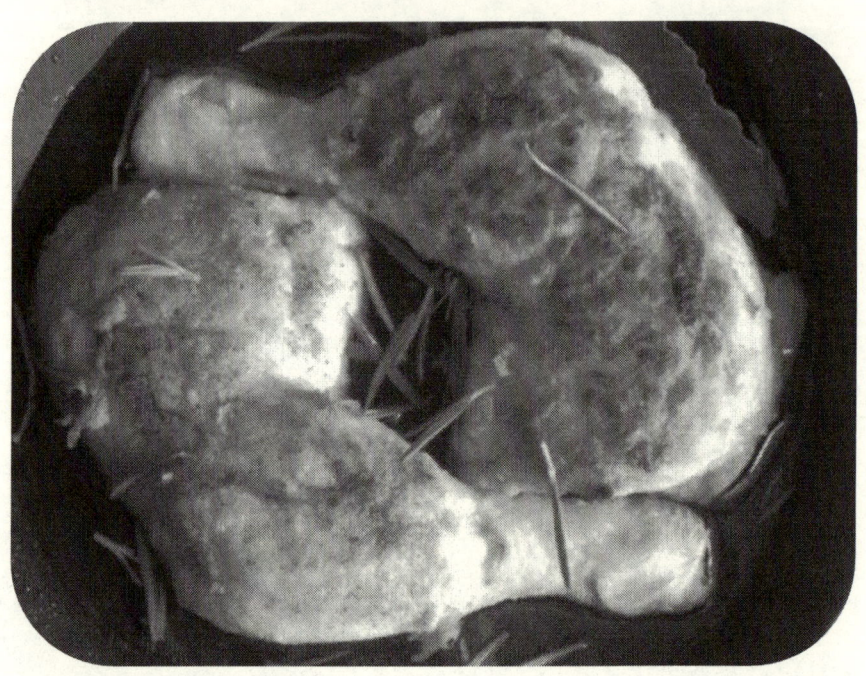

Prep Time: 25 minutes

Servings: 2

INGREDIENTS
- Chicken legs 4
- Coarse salt to taste
- Ground black pepper to taste
- Wheat flour 3.5 oz.
- Extra virgin olive oil 50 ml
- White wine 220 ml
- Fresh rosemary 3 stems

- Bay leaves 2
- Lemon juice 20 ml

COOKING INSTRUCTIONS

1. Preheat the oven to 430 degrees F. Rub the skin of the chicken legs with salt and pepper on all sides. Sift flour into a large dish and roll chicken legs in it.
2. Heat oil in a refractory pan and fry the meat over medium heat for 10 minutes on both sides until a golden crust appears. Then pour in the wine, toss in the rosemary and bay leaves, and boil the liquid for 2 minutes. Then pour in one and a half glasses of water, bring to a boil, and remove from heat.
3. Cover the pan and place in the oven for 45 minutes. Remove the lid and leave in the oven for another 5 minutes.
4. Remove the chicken legs from the oven, pour lemon juice into the pan, mix, and serve the chicken with the sauce from the bottom of the pan.

CHAPTER 5 «DINNER RECIPES»

The dinner meal differs in importance, its ingredients, and schedule from one culture to another. There are those who prepare it as a basic, indispensable meal, and there are those who never eat it. There are many special kitchens in each culture and the most delicious foods and dishes served during this meal can be dazzling.

Dinner Before Bed

When should you stop eating dinner?
Research on this topic is unable to agree on a specific time when it's advisable to stop eating, but they agree that it is not recommended to eat food fewer than three hours before bedtime. The body needs three hours to digest food when eating a meal with moderate calories, so the solution to not feeling hungry late at night is to get the necessary calories for your body earlier in the day. In addition to eating at least 30 grams of protein in one serving, it helps to eat six small meals a day instead of three big meals.

Early Dinner

There are many benefits to eating dinner early. It helps those trying to get a beautiful body and slimmer waist because it allows the body to burn calories faster, smoother, and more efficiently. Routine movement, such as walking or climbing stairs facilitate digestion and burn calories.

For better sleep, do not eat dinner late at night. It can cause indigestion, which leads to trouble sleeping, as heavy meals and alcohol are both things that one should not ingest before bed. They can deprive you of the pleasure of deep sleep and cause several sleep-related disorders in the long run.

People who eat late at night show a need to eat more later. Studies also indicate that eating late at night raises the percentage of triglycerides in the body. This is because the calories that are not immediately burned convert into triglycerides, and these fats can become dangerous in high levels, leading to heart attacks and strokes.

CROWN ROAST OF PORK WITH MUSHROOM DRESSING

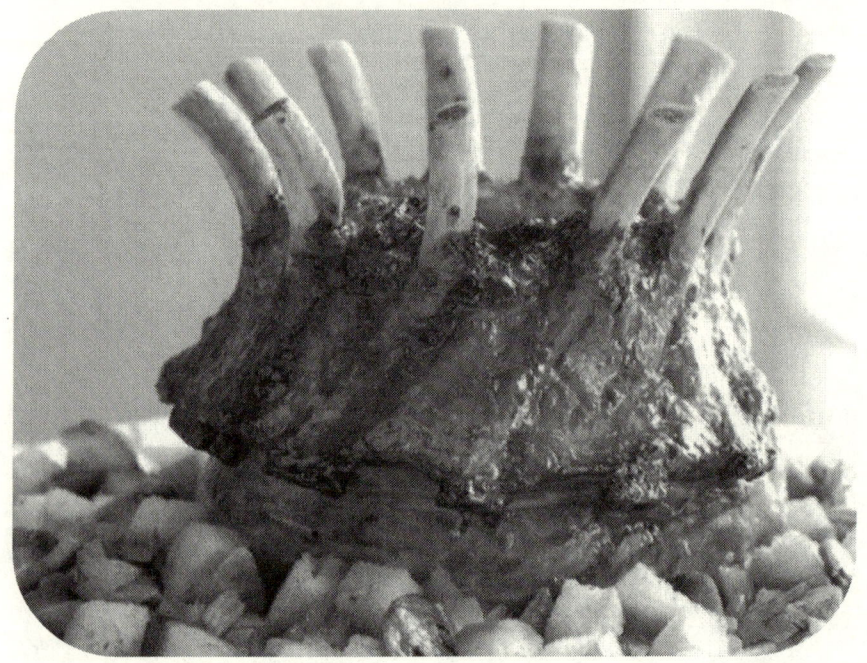

Prep Time: 15 minutes.

Bake: 1 hour and 15 minutes.

Servings: 10

INGREDIENTS
- 1 roast pork (10 to 12 rows of ribs, about 6 to 8 pounds)
- 1/2 teaspoon marinated salt

Mushroom dressing:
- 1/4 cup butter
- 1 cup chopped fresh mushrooms
- 1/2 cup chopped celery
- 3 cups toasted bread
- 1/4 teaspoon salt
- 1/4 teaspoon pepper
- 1/3 cup apricots
- 1 cup fresh cranberries, optional

COOKING INSTRUCTIONS

1. Preheat the oven to 350 degrees F. Place the rib ends of the oven in a shallow baking dish. Sprinkle with marinated salt. Cover the rib ends with paper. Bake for 1 hour and 15 minutes.
2. At the same time, melt the butter over medium heat. Add mushrooms and celery. Fry until tender. Add bread, salt, and pepper. Heat together. Bake until the thermometer inserted into the meat between the ribs shows a reading of 300 degrees F for 45-60 minutes. Remove the foil. Let the meat sit for 10 minutes before slicing.
3. If necessary, thread the cranberry through 20 inches of string or thread. Transfer the ribs to a plate. The cranberry links are on the inside and outside of the ribs. Slice between the ribs and serve.

BACON-WRAPPED PESTO PORK TENDERLOIN

Prep Time: 30 minutes.

Bake: 20 minutes.

Servings: 4

INGREDIENTS
- 10 slices of bacon
- 1 pork tenderloin (1 pound)
- 1/4 teaspoon pepper
- 1/3 cup pesto

- 1 cup grated Italian cheese
- 1 cup fresh spinach

COOKING INSTRUCTIONS

1. Preheat the oven to 425 degrees F. Arrange the bacon strips vertically on a 15" x 10" foil-lined frying pan (they will overlap slightly).
2. Cut the pork tenderloin 1/2 inch from the bottom along the length. Open the tenderloin. Beat it to 1/2 inch thickness with a meat hammer. Place the tenderloin in the center of the bacon, perpendicular to the strips of meat.
3. Sprinkle pepper on the pork. Coat with pesto. Layer with cheese and spinach. Wrap with bacon and tuck at both ends. Bundle with kitchen floss. Use toothpicks at the ends to lock.
4. Place in frying pan, brown on all sides for about 8 minutes. Return to the baking tray. Bake in the oven until the pork thermometer reaches 250 degrees F for 17-20 minutes. Remove floss and toothpicks; let us stand for 5 minutes before cutting.

PRIME RIB WITH FRESH HERB SAUCE

Prep Time: 40 minutes.

Bake: 3-1/4 hours + standing time.

Servings: 10 (1-1/2 cups sauce)

INGREDIENTS
- 1 prime rib (6 to 8 pounds)
- 1 teaspoon coarse salt
- 1 teaspoon freshly ground pepper
- 3 glasses of water

- 2 small onions, cut in half
- 7 cloves of garlic
- 5 fresh sage branches
- 5 fresh thyme branches
- 2 bay leaves

Herb sauce:
- 2 tablespoons butter
- 2 leeks, thinly sliced
- 4 cloves garlic, thinly sliced
- 5 fresh sage branches
- 5 fresh thyme branches
- 2 bay leaves
- 1 tablespoon all-purpose flour
- 2 tablespoons black pepper
- 1/4 teaspoon coarse salt
- 1-1/2 to 2-1/2 cups of separate broth
- 1/2 cup red wine or dried broth
- 1/2 teaspoon red wine vinegar
- fresh thyme branches, optional

COOKING INSTRUCTIONS

1. Preheat the oven to 450 degrees F. Place the meat in a shallow baking tray with the fat facing up, rub with salt and pepper. Add 1 cup of water, onion, garlic, and herbs to the baking dish. Bake for 15 minutes.

2. Lower the oven setting to 325 degrees F. Bake for 3 to 3-1/2 hours or more until the meat reaches the desired maturity level. Add 1 cup of water per hour.

3. For the herb sauce, heat the butter in a large saucepan over medium heat. Add shallots. Boil and stir for 5-6 minutes or until soft. Add garlic and herbs. Cook for another minute. Add flour, pepper, and salt and mix. Gradually add 1/2 cup of soup stock and remove from heat.

4. Before carving, let meat stand for 15 minutes. At the same time, filter all juice through a sieve in a measuring cup. Get rid of onions and herbs. Filter the fat from the juice. If necessary, add more soup to the frying juice to measure a cup. Add the leek mixture.

5. Place the baking tray on both burners. Add wine. Boil. Cook for 2-3 minutes, stirring to loosen the brown pieces in the pan. Add sauce. Bring to a boil, stirring occasionally. Cook until the mixture drops about 1-1/2 cups for 10-15 minutes.

6. Stir with vinegar. Strain, get rid of leeks and herbs. Add thyme as needed.

DUCK BREASTS WITH APRICOT CHUTNEY

Prep Time: 30 minutes.

Bake: 30 minutes + cooling time.

Servings: 12

INGREDIENTS
- 1-1/2 cups orange juice
- 2/3 cup sugar
- 2 packages (6 ounces each) dried apricots, chopped
- 1/2 cup dried cherries
- 1/2 cup golden raisins

- 2 teaspoons minced fresh ginger root
- 3/4 teaspoon ground cilantro
- 3/4 teaspoon ground cumin
- 1/4 teaspoon salt
- 1/4 teaspoon pepper
- 1/8 teaspoon ground cloves
- 2 teaspoons lemon juice

Duck:
- 12 duck breasts with skin (5 ounces each)
- 1-1/2 teaspoons salt
- 1/4 teaspoon pepper
- 2 tablespoons olive oil

Orange sauce:
- 1/4 teaspoon minced garlic
- 1/2 cup Marsala wine
- 1/2 teaspoon cornstarch
- 1/2 cup orange juice
- 1/3 cup chicken broth
- 2 tablespoons grated orange zest
- 3 tablespoons cold butter
- 1 tablespoon minced fresh basil

COOKING INSTRUCTIONS

1. To make the chutney, combine orange juice and sugar in a saucepan. Cook and stir over medium heat until sugar

is dissolved, about 3 minutes. Add the apricots, cherries, raisins, ginger, cilantro, cumin, salt, pepper, and cloves. Bring to a boil. Reduce heat to low. Cook until apricots are tender, about 10 minutes. Transfer to a bowl; stir in lemon juice. Let stand at room temperature for at least 2 hours.

2. Season both sides of duck with salt and pepper. In a large skillet, sauté duck (skin side down) in oil until skin is browned. Turn and cook for 1 minute. Set aside 1 tablespoon of drippings.

3. Place duck on a greased rack in a shallow roasting pan. Bake at 350 degrees F until meat reaches desired doneness: 30-35 minutes.

4. For orange sauce, sauté garlic in reserved drippings for 1 minute. Add wine, bring to a boil. Cook and stir until reduced by half. In a bowl, combine the cornstarch, orange juice, broth, and orange zest until blended. Stir into wine mixture. Bring to a boil. Reduce heat. Simmer uncovered for 5 minutes. Remove from the heat. Add butter and basil; whisk until smooth. Remove skin from duck before slicing, if desired. Serve with orange sauce and chutney.

PORK TENDERLOIN WITH THREE-BERRY SALSA

INGREDIENTS
- 1-1/4 cups of fresh or frozen blackberries (about 6 ounces)
- 1-1/4 cups of fresh or frozen raspberries (about 6 ounces)
- 1 cup melted fresh or frozen blueberries (about 6 ounces)
- 1 medium sweet red pepper, chopped
- 1 jalapeno, chopped
- 1/2 medium red onion, chopped
- 1/4 cup lemon juice
- 3 tablespoons chopped fresh cilantro
- 1/4 teaspoon salt

Pork:
- 2 pork chops (3/4 pounds each) cut into 3/4 inch slices
- 1 teaspoon salt
- 1/2 teaspoon pepper
- 2 tablespoons olive oil
- 1/2 cup white wine or chicken broth
- 2 leeks, thinly sliced
- 1/2 cup chicken broth

COOKING INSTRUCTIONS

1. Put the first five ingredients in a bowl. Gently toss to merge. Keep a cup of raspberry mixture as a seasoning. For the sauce, gently stir the onion, lemon juice, cilantro, and salt into the remaining mixture. Let stand for 30 minutes.
2. Meanwhile, sprinkle the pork with salt and pepper. In a large frying pan, heat a tablespoon of oil over medium heat. Add half of the pork and cook until the temperature of the pork thermometer reads 290 degrees F, 2-4 minutes on each side. Remove from the pan. Repeat with the remaining pork and oil.
3. Mix the wine, leeks, and preserved berries together and put in the pot, stirring to loosen the brown part. Boil. Cook for 4-6 minutes. Return the pork to the pan. Serve with sauce.

ITALIAN ROULADE

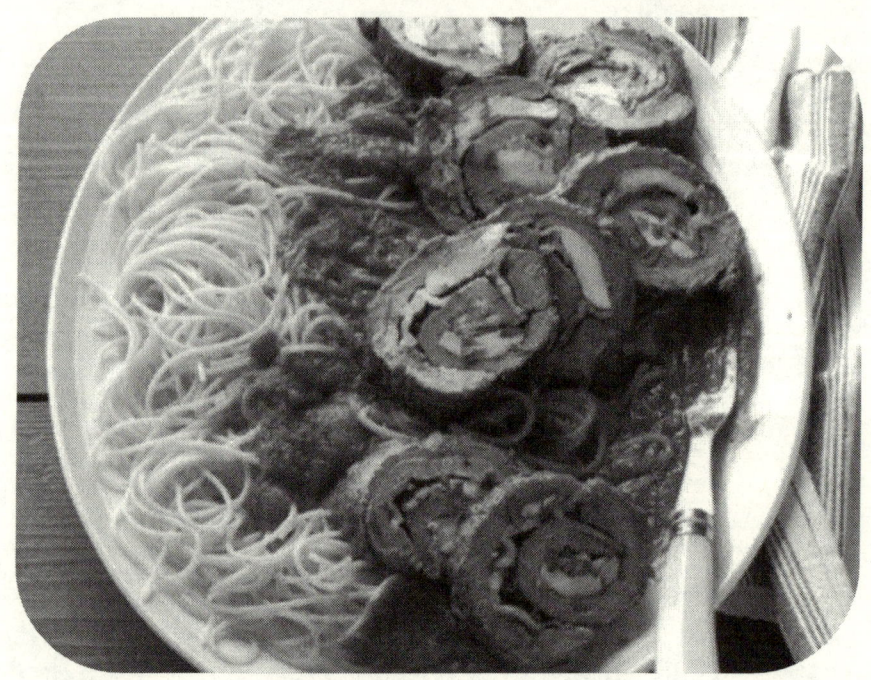

Prep Time: 30 minutes.

Cook Time: 1-1/2 hours.

Servings: 8

INGREDIENTS
- Slices of bacon 6
- Chopped cloves garlic 2
- Italian spices 3/4 tsp
- Salt 1/2 tsp
- Pepper 1/2 tsp
- 1 steak (1-1/2 to 2 pounds)

- Grated Parmesan cheese 1/4 cup
- 3 large boiled eggs, cut into thin slices
- Chopped fresh parsley 1/4 cup
- Olive oil 2 tblp
- Beef pasta sauce 3 cans (24 ounces each)
- Hot pasta
- Chopped fresh parsley

COOKING INSTRUCTIONS

1. Preheat the oven to 350 degrees F. Place the bacon on a microwave-safe bowl lined with paper towels. Cover with extra paper towels; microwave in high temperature for 3-5 minutes, or until partially cooked but not crispy. In a small bowl, mix garlic, Italian spices, salt, and pepper.

2. Starting from the long side, cut the meat horizontally to half an inch from the other side. Use a meat hammer to open the steak to 1/4 inch thickness.

3. Sprinkle the garlic mixture on the steak. Sprinkle with cheese. Layer eggs and bacon within 1 inch of the edge; sprinkle with cilantro. Starting from the long side of the steak, roll along the grain and tie at 1-1/2 inches with thread.

4. Heat the oil at a medium-high temperature in a Dutch oven. Brown meat rolls in all directions. Pour pasta

sauce. Bake and cover 1-1/2 to 1-3/4 hours or until the meat is tender.

5. Remove the meat roll from the bowl. Remove the thread and cut the roll into strips. Serve with pasta sauce. Sprinkle with extra cilantro.

WHOLE BALSAMIC ROAST CHICKEN

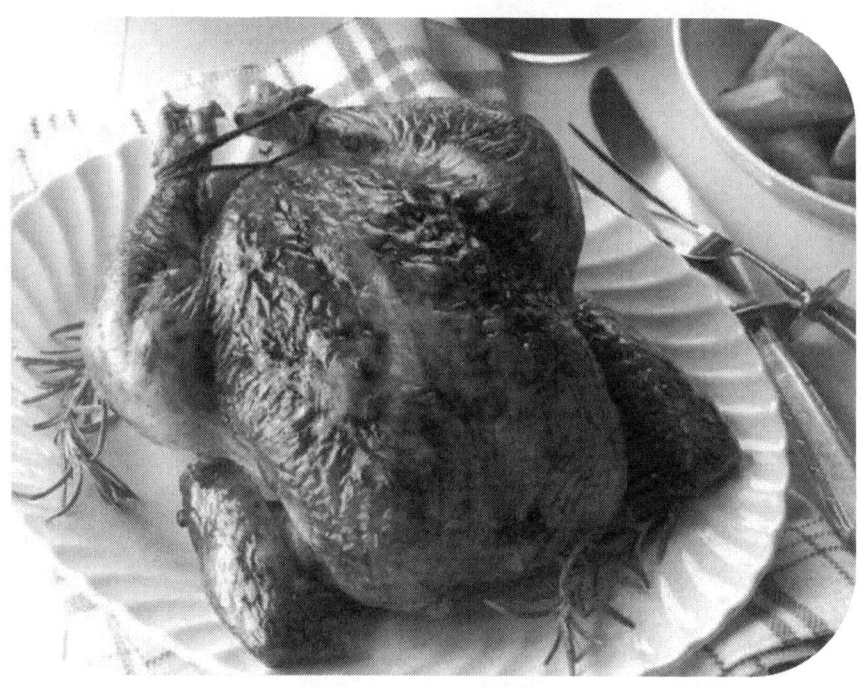

Prep Time: 20 minutes.

Bake: 2 hours + standing time.

Servings: 12 (1-1/2 cups onion sauce)

INGREDIENTS
- 2 tablespoons chopped fresh rosemary or 2 teaspoons chopped dried rosemary
- 3 cloves minced garlic
- 1 teaspoon salt
- 1 teaspoon ground pepper

- 2 chopped medium red onions
- 1 roast chicken (6 to 7 pounds)
- 1/2 cup dry wine or low-sodium chicken broth
- 1/2 cup balsamic vinegar

COOKING INSTRUCTIONS

1. Preheat the oven to 350 degrees F. Mix rosemary, garlic, salt, and pepper. Place the onions in the frying pan.
2. Pat chicken dry. Use your fingers to loosen the chicken skin carefully and rub the rosemary mixture under the skin. Use a toothpick to secure the skin to the bottom of the breast. Tuck chicken wings under the chicken, tie thighs together.
3. Mix wine and vinegar. Pour it over the chicken. Bake for 2 to 2 1/2 hours or until a thermometer inserted into the thicker part of the thigh reads 170 -175 degrees.
4. Remove the chicken from the oven. Before carving, let stand for 15 minutes. Transfer onion and broth to a small bowl; no fat. Before serving, remove the skin from the chicken. Serve with onion sauce.

SLOW-SIMMERED BEEF STEW

Prep Time: 30 minutes.

Bake: 1-3/4 hours.

Servings: 4

INGREDIENTS
- 1-1/2 pounds of cooked beef (1-1/4 inch pieces)
- 3 teaspoons multi-purpose flour
- 3/4 teaspoon salt
- 2 to 4 teaspoons canola oil

- 2 teaspoons broth
- 2 teaspoons dried parsley
- 1-1/2 teaspoons Italian spices
- 2 glasses of water
- 1 cup Burgundy wine or broth
- 3 medium-sized potatoes (about 1-1/3 pounds), peeled and cut into quarters
- 1 cup fresh mushrooms, halved
- 1 medium-sized onion, cut into 8 wedges
- 2 medium carrots, cut into 1-inch pieces
- 2 celery ribs, cut into 1/2-inch pieces
- Extra water, optional

COOKING INSTRUCTIONS

1. Preheat the oven to 350 degrees F. Lightly cover the fried meat with flour and salt. Eliminate excess. In an oven resistant Dutch oven, heat 2 tablespoons of oil over medium heat. Add the brown beef in batches and other oils as needed. Remove from the pan.
2. Add broth, herbs, 2 cups of water, and the wine to the same frying pan. Bring to a boil and stir to loosen the brown pieces of the pot. Re-boil the beef. Transfer to the oven, cover for 1 hour.
3. Add vegetables and sprinkle with additional water as needed. Bake for 45-60 minutes until the beef and vegetables are tender.

PINEAPPLE HAM WITH BROWN SUGAR

Prep Time: 10 minutes.

Bake: 2 hours.

Servings: 12

INGREDIENTS
- 1 whole cooked ham (7 to 9 pounds)
- 1 can (20 ounces) crushed pineapple
- 1 cup packed brown sugar
- 1 tablespoon Dijon mustard
- 1/4 teaspoon cloves

COOKING INSTRUCTIONS

1. Preheat the oven to 325 degrees F. Place the ham on a shelf in a shallow roasting bowl. Use a sharp knife to cut the surface with a 1/2 inch diamond cut. Cover and bake for 1-1/2 hours.

2. In a small bowl, mix the remaining ingredients. Spread over the ham and then press the mixture into small pieces. Roast it uncovered for 30-60 minutes or until the thermometer reads 280 degrees F.

DAD'S FAMOUS STUFFIES

Prep Time: 1-1/4 hours.

Bake: 20 minutes.

Servings: 10 (3 clams each)

INGREDIENTS
- 20 large oysters (about 10 pounds)
- 1 pound of smoked Portuguese sausage or fully-cooked Spanish sausage
- 1 large onion, chopped (about 2 cups)
- 3 teaspoons sea spices
- 1 pack (14 ounces) herbal filling cubes

- 1 cup of water
- Lemon wedges, optional
- Chili sauce, optional

COOKING INSTRUCTIONS

1. Add 2 inches of water to the pan. Add oysters and sausage. Boil. Cover and steam for 15-20 minutes or until the shellfish opens.
2. Remove oysters and sausages from the pan and save 2 cups of cooking liquid. Get rid of any unopened oysters.
3. Preheat the oven to 350 degrees F. Remove oyster meat from the shell. Retain 30 half shells for filling. Chop clams in the food processor. Transfer to a large bowl.
4. Remove the casing from the sausage. Cut the sausage into 1-1/2 inch pieces. Chop in a food processor. Add sausage, onion, and seafood sauce to the chopped oysters. Add herbal filling cubes. Add the reserved cooking liquid and enough water to achieve the required humidity, about 1 cup.
5. Place the oyster mixture into the reserved shells. Bake until heated for 15-20 minutes. Preheat broiler.
6. Shellfish will burn 4-6 inches before being heated for 4-5 minutes or until golden brown. If needed, it can be eaten with lemon slices and pepper sauce.

7. Freezing option: Cover and freeze grilled shellfish. Transfer to a freezer container. Place in the freezer. When using, put 3 oysters into a microwave-safe plate. Cover with paper towels. Heat in the microwave on high for 3-4 minutes. Follow the instructions.

ASPARAGUS CLUB ROULADES

Prep Time: 20 minutes.

Cook: 15 minutes.

Servings: 8

INGREDIENTS
- 3/4 pound fresh asparagus
- 8 pieces of turkey breast (about 1 pound)
- 1 tablespoon Dijon mayonnaise mix
- 8 slices provolone

- 8 slices ham
- 1/2 teaspoon poultry seasoning
- 1/2 teaspoon pepper
- 8 slices of bacon

Sauce:
- 2/3 cup Dijon mayonnaise
- 4 teaspoons 2% milk
- 1/4 teaspoon poultry seasoning

COOKING INSTRUCTIONS

1. Boil 4 cups of water in a large pot. Add asparagus. Cook (not covered) for 3 minutes or until soft. Filter the asparagus into ice water immediately. Drain the water.
2. Spread turkey slices with Dijon mayonnaise. Layer ham, cheese, and asparagus. Sprinkle with poultry and pepper spices. Roll tightly, then roll with bacon.
3. Cook in a large pot over medium to high heat until the bacon becomes crispy and the turkey is no longer pink, sometimes it takes 12-15 minutes. Combine the ingredients of the sauce. Serve with meat rolls.

SALMON FILLETS STUFFED BY SEAFOOD

Prep Time: 25 minutes.

Bake: 20 minutes.

Servings: 12

INGREDIENTS
- 1-1/2 cups of rice
- 1 packet (8 ounces) of imitation crab meat
- 2 tablespoons soft cream cheese
- 2 tablespoons melted butter

- 2 cloves garlic, chopped
- 1/2 teaspoon each of grated dried basil, oregano, thyme, oregano, and rosemary
- 1/2 teaspoon celery seeds, grated
- 12 salmon fillets (8 ounces each, 1-1/2 inches thick)
- 3 tablespoons olive oil
- 2 teaspoons dill
- 1-1/2 teaspoons salt

COOKING INSTRUCTIONS

1. Preheat the oven to 400 degrees F. In a large bowl, mix rice, crab, cream cheese, butter, garlic, basil, oregano, thyme, rosemary, and celery seeds.
2. In each slice, cut a half-inch pocket from the opposite side. Stuff with filling mixture and close with a toothpick. Place salmon on oiled baking dish. Brush with oil and sprinkle with dill and salt.
3. Bake for 18-22 minutes or until the fish begins to flake easily with a fork. Remove toothpicks before serving.

RACK OF LAMB

Prep Time: 10 minutes.

Bake: 30 minutes.

Servings: 4

INGREDIENTS
- 2 lamb racks (1-1/2 pounds each)
- 1/4 cup grated lemon zest
- 1/4 cup chopped oregano or 4 teaspoons oregano
- 6 cloves minced garlic
- 1 tablespoon olive oil
- 1/4 teaspoon salt

- 1/4 teaspoon pepper
- Sliced fresh oregano and lemon, optional

COOKING INSTRUCTIONS

1. Preheat the oven to 375 degrees F. Place the lamb in a shallow frying pan. In a small bowl, mix lemon zest, oregano, garlic, oil, salt, and pepper. Rub this over the lamb.
2. Bake for 30 to 40 minutes or until the meat reaches the required maturity level. Leave it for 5 minutes before cutting. If needed, it can be eaten with fresh oregano and lemon slices.

BEEF TENDERLOIN STUFFED BY ARTICHOKE

Prep Time: 30 minutes.

Bake: 40 minutes + standing time.

Servings: 10

INGREDIENTS
- 1 chopped medium onion
- 3 cloves minced garlic
- 1/4 cup butter
- 1 box (14 ounces) of artichoke hearts in water, rinsed, dried and cut into pieces

- 2 cans (6 ounces each) of mushroom slices, drained
- 1-1/2 cups of chicken soup
- 1 pack (6 ounces) filling mixture
- 1 piece of roasted soft beef (3 to 3-1/2 pounds)
- 4 slices of bacon, cut in half

COOKING INSTRUCTIONS

1. In a large frying pan, fry the onions and garlic in butter. Add artichokes, mushrooms, and gravy. Boil. Keep away from heat. Stir in the filling mixture. Let cool.
2. Cut a longitudinal slit down the center of the tenderloin so that it is 1/2 inch from the bottom. Open the loin until flat. In each half, cut a half inch further from the center down. Turn on the roaster and cover with plastic wrap. Flatten to 1/2 inch thickness. Remove the plastic.
3. Sprinkle the filling on the meat. Roll up from the long side. Secure the grill at 2 inches. Tie off with thread. Place it in a shallow baking bowl; place the bacon slices on the grill.
4. Bake at 425 degrees F for 40 to 50 minutes, or until the meat reaches the required maturity. Let it rest for 10 minutes before cutting.

ROAST DUCKLING WITH CRANBERRY AND ORANGE

Prep Time: 20 minutes.

Bake: 3 hours + standing time.

Servings: 10

INGREDIENTS
- 2 ducklings (4 to 5 pounds)
- 2 medium-sized oranges, fried in quarters
- 2 fresh rosemary sprigs
- 1-1/2 cups fresh or frozen cranberries separately
- 4 glasses of orange juice

- 1 cup chicken broth
- 1/4 cup soy sauce
- 2 teaspoons sugar
- 2 cloves garlic, chopped
- 1 teaspoon grated fresh ginger
- 2/3 cup jam

COOKING INSTRUCTIONS

1. Preheat the oven to 350 degrees F. Put 4 oranges, rosemary branch, and 1/4 cup cranberries in each duck cavity. Tie thighs together. Place on baking tray with the breast side up.
2. In a bowl, mix orange juice, broth, soy sauce, sugar, garlic, and ginger. Place half a cup in the refrigerator. Pour 1 cup onto the duckling. Sprinkle with remaining cranberries. Cover and bake for 1 hour. Test and bake for 1-1/2 hours, and stir repeatedly with the remaining orange juice mixture. (Pile up fat and drain it from the pan.)
3. Mix jam and preserved orange juice mixture. Pour over young ducks. Bake until exposed, until the thermometer on the thigh reads 180 degrees F for 30-40 minutes. Remove oranges, rosemary, and cranberries from the cavity. Let the duckling stand for 10 minutes before carving.

RAVIOLI WITH TOMATO SAUCE

Prep Time: 2 hours.

Cook: 10 minutes.

Servings: 6

INGREDIENTS
- 6 to 6-1/2 cups all-purpose flour
- 6 large eggs
- 3/4 cup water
- 2 teaspoons olive oil

Sauce:
- 1 can (28 ounces) mashed potatoes
- 1-1/2 cups tomato paste
- 1/2 cup grated Parmesan cheese
- 1/3 cup water
- 1/3 cup tomato paste
- 3 tablespoons sugar
- 2 tablespoons fresh chopped basil
- 1 tablespoon chopped cilantro
- 1 tablespoon fresh minced spices
- 1 clove garlic, chopped
- 1/2 teaspoon of salt
- 1/4 teaspoon pepper

Filling:
- 1 can (15 ounces) ricotta cheese
- 2 cups chopped mozzarella cheese
- 1/3 cup grated Parmesan cheese
- 1 large egg, beat a little
- 2 teaspoons chopped fresh basil
- 1 teaspoon chopped fresh parsley
- 1 teaspoon freshly chopped oregano
- 1/4 teaspoon garlic powder
- 1/8 teaspoon salt
- 1/8 teaspoon ground pepper

COOKING INSTRUCTIONS

1. Place 6 cups of flour in a large bowl. Beat eggs, water, and oil. Pour into a well in the center of the flour. Mix to form a ball, knead for about 8-10 minutes until smooth and elastic, adding remaining flour if necessary to prevent the dough from sticking. Cover it and let it sit for 30 minutes.

2. Meanwhile, in a Dutch oven, mix the ingredients of the sauce. Boil. Reduce the heat, cover the mixture, and simmer for an hour, stirring occasionally.

3. In a large bowl, mix the filling. Cover and cool until ready to use.

4. Divide the pasta dough into four equal parts. Wrap a portion to 1/16 inch thickness. (Cover the pasta until it is ready for use.) Work quickly, putting 1 teaspoon of 1-inch filling in each one. Clean with water to moisturize. Fold the dough, press to close. Cut into squares with pastry wheels. Repeat with the remaining dough and fill.

5. Boil the brine kettle. Add ravioli. Reduce heat and cook for 1-2 minutes or until the ravioli rises and softens.

TIKKA MASALA WITH CHICKEN

Prep Time: 25 minutes.

Cook: 4-1/4 hours.

Servings: 8

INGREDIENTS
- 1 can (29 ounces) tomato paste
- 1-1/2 cups plain yogurt
- 1/2 large onion, chopped
- 2 tablespoons olive oil
- 4-1/2 teaspoons chopped fresh ginger

- ➤ 4 cloves minced garlic
- ➤ 1 tablespoon garam masala
- ➤ 2-1/2 teaspoons salt
- ➤ 1-1/2 teaspoons cumin powder
- ➤ 1 teaspoon paprika
- ➤ 3/4 teaspoon pepper
- ➤ 1/2 teaspoon chili
- ➤ 1/4 teaspoon ground cinnamon
- ➤ 2-1/2 pounds boneless skinless chicken breast cut into 1-1/2 inch cubes
- ➤ 1 jalapeño
- ➤ 1 bay leaf
- ➤ 1 tablespoon cornstarch
- ➤ 1 cup heavy cream
- ➤ Basmati rice
- ➤ Chopped fresh cilantro, optional

COOKING INSTRUCTIONS

1. Place the first 13 ingredients in a 5 quart slow-cooker. Add chicken, jalapeño, and bay leaf. Cook, cover the pot, and reduce the heat for 4 hours or until the chicken is tender. Remove jalapeño and bay leaf.
2. In a small bowl, mix cornstarch and cream evenly. Gradually add sauce. Heat and cook for 15-20 minutes or until the sauce thickens. Serve with rice. Sprinkle cilantro if needed.

PORK TENDERLOIN WITH SPINACH

Prep Time: 25 minutes.

Bake: 25 minutes + standing time.

Servings: 4

INGREDIENTS

- 2 cups shredded spinach
- 1/4 cup water
- 1/2 cup frozen artichoke hearts, chopped
- 1/3 cup Parmesan cheese

- 1/4 teaspoon dried rosemary
- 1 pork tenderloin (1 pound)
- 1/2 teaspoon salt
- 1/8 teaspoon ground pepper

Sauce:
- 1/2 cup cranberry juice
- 1/4 cup balsamic vinegar
- 1 tablespoon sugar

COOKING INSTRUCTIONS

1. In a large cast iron skillet or other oven, boil spinach in water over medium heat for 3-4 minutes until wilted. Drain well. In a large bowl, mix spinach, artichokes, parmesan cheese, and rosemary.
2. Cut the center of the longitudinal slit in half on the inside of the bottom. Open the meat until it settles. Cover with plastic wrap. Flatten to 1/4 inch thickness; remove plastic. Sprinkle 1/4 teaspoon salt on the meat. Place the spinach mixture on top.
3. Bind the meat with a kitchen thread and secure the end with a toothpick. Sprinkle with pepper and remaining salt. Put it in the pan. Bake at 425 degrees F for 15 minutes.

4. Meanwhile, in a small saucepan, mix the seasoning. Boil the mixture on medium heat. Reduce heat and expose to slow fire for 15 minutes. Pour it over the meat. Bake until the thermometer reads 145 degrees and extend for another 10 minutes. Leave it for 10 minutes before cutting. Remove toothpicks.

LEMONY SALMON PATTIES

Prep Time: 20 minutes.

Bake: 45 minutes.

Servings: 4

INGREDIENTS
- 1 box (14-3/4 ounces) of pink salmon, light yellow, with skin and bones removed
- 3/4 cup whole milk
- 1 cup soft bread crumbs

- 1 large egg, beat a little
- 1 tablespoon chopped cilantro
- 1 teaspoon chopped onion
- 1/2 teaspoon Worcestershire sauce
- 1/4 teaspoon salt
- 1/8 teaspoon ground pepper

Lemon sauce:
- 2 tablespoons butter
- 4 teaspoons all-purpose flour
- 3/4 cup whole milk
- 2 tablespoons lemon juice
- 1/4 teaspoon salt
- 1/8 to 1/4 teaspoon chili

COOKING INSTRUCTIONS

1. Preheat the oven to 350 degrees F. In a large bowl, mix the first nine ingredients. Fill 8 muffin cups with a quarter of this salmon mixture. Bake for 45 minutes or until brown.

2. At the same time, melt the butter in the pan. Add flour and stir until smooth. Stir the milk gradually and bring to a boil over medium heat. Stir for 2 minutes or until thickened, remove from heat. Add lemon juice, salt, and chili. Serve with patties.

BEEF CHUCK ROAST (SLOW-COOKER)

Prep Time: 20 minutes.

Cook: 6 hours.

Servings: 8

INGREDIENTS
- 14 ounces ketchup
- 1 onion, chopped
- 3/4 cup packed brown sugar
- 3/4 cup cider vinegar
- 1 tablespoon mixed pickling spices

- 3 bay leaves
- 1 boneless beef chuck roast or rump roast (3 to 4 pounds)
- 4 cups water
- 1-1/2 cups crushed gingersnap cookies (about 30 cookies)
- 2 tablespoons cornstarch
- 1/4 cup cold water

COOKING INSTRUCTIONS

1. Mix first six ingredients. Place roast in a 5 quart slow cooker, add water. Pour ketchup mixture over top. Add cookie crumbs. Cover and cook on low until meat is tender, 6-8 hours.
2. Remove roast from slow cooker, keep warm. Strain cooking juices and skim fat. Transfer 4 cups juices to a saucepan and bring to a boil. Mix cornstarch and water until smooth, stir into cooking juices. Return to a boil. Cook and stir until thickened, 1-2 minutes. Serve with roast.

SHREDDED BARBECUE CHICKEN OVER GRITS

Prep. Time: 20 minutes.

Cook: 25 minutes.

Servings: 6

INGREDIENTS

- 1 pound boneless, skinless chicken breast
- 1/4 teaspoon pepper
- 1 box (14-1/2 oz.) sodium chicken broth

- 1 cup pecan smoked barbecue sauce
- 1/4 cup syrup
- 1 tablespoon chili
- 1/2 teaspoon ground cinnamon
- 2-1/4 glasses of water
- 1 cup semolina for quick cooking
- 1 cup canned pumpkin
- 3/4 cup chopped pepper jack cheese
- 1 medium-sized tomato, chopped
- 6 tablespoons sour cream
- 2 chopped green onions
- 2 tablespoons chopped fresh cilantro

COOKING INSTRUCTIONS

1. Sprinkle pepper on the chicken. Place it in a large non-stick pan with cooking spray.
2. In a large bowl, mix 1 cup of broth, barbecue sauce, molasses, chili, and cinnamon. Pour it on the chicken. Boil. Reduce the heat, cover, and simmer for 20-25 minutes or until the thermometer reads 330 degrees F. Use two forks to chop the meat and put it back in the pot.
3. Meanwhile, in a large pot, boil the remaining water and broth. Slowly stir the grits and the pumpkin. Cook hot

and stir for 5-7 minutes or until thickened. Add cheese until melted.

4. Divide the grits into 6 portions and add a half cup of chicken over each. Serve with tomatoes, sour cream, green onions, and parsley.

MUSHROOM-STUFFED FLANK STEAK ROLL

Prep Time: 25 minutes.

Marinating Bake: 1-1/4 hours + standing time.

Servings: 6

INGREDIENTS
- 1 flank steak (about 1-1/2 pounds)
- 1/2 cup lemon juice
- 1/2 cup soy sauce
- 1/2 cup honey

- 2 teaspoons mustard
- 1 teaspoon ground pepper
- 1/2 teaspoon grated lemon zest, optional

Mushroom stuffing:
- 1 pound fresh mushroom slices
- 1 medium onion, chopped
- 1/4 cup butter
- 1/2 cup chopped fresh parsley
- 2 tablespoons cornstarch
- 2 cups beef broth

COOKING INSTRUCTIONS

1. Cut the meat horizontally from the long side to half an inch on the other side. Open the flank steak, cover with plastic wrap. Flatten to 1/4 inch thickness.

2. In a small bowl, mix lemon juice, soy sauce, honey, mustard, pepper, and sprinkle with lemon if needed. Pour half of the marinade into a shallow dish. Add beef and coat it with the marinade. Cover and let cool overnight. Cover the remaining mixture and place in the refrigerator.

3. In a large frying pan, sauté mushrooms and onions in butter. Remove from heat. Stir in the cilantro. Drain and remove marinade. Open the steak and spoon on the mushroom stuffing. Starting from the long side, roll up

tightly. Bundle with kitchen thread. Place it in a shallow baking pan. Pour the seasoning over the steak roll.

4. Cover and bake at 350 degrees F for 45 minutes. Uncover and bake for 30 minutes more, or until the meat reaches the required maturity. Remove from heat. Transfer the cooking juice to a pot and remove the fat. Cook the juice, bring to a boil. Mix in corn starch and broth until smooth. Cook and stir for 1-2 minutes or until thickened. Cut the meat into thin slices. Serve with the sauce.

CLASSIC CRAB CAKES

Prep Time: 20 minutes.

Servings: 8

INGREDIENTS

- 1 pound fresh or canned crab (shelled, peeled, and cartilage removed)
- 2 to 2-1/2 cups of soft crumbs
- 1 large egg, beaten
- 3/4 cup mayonnaise
- 1/3 cup chopped celery, green pepper, and onion
- 1 tablespoon sea spices

- 1 tablespoon chopped cilantro
- 2 teaspoons lemon juice
- 1 teaspoon Worcestershire sauce
- 1 teaspoon mustard
- 1/4 teaspoon pepper
- 1/8 teaspoon chili sauce
- 2 to 4 tablespoons vegetable oil, optional
- Lemon wedges, optional

COOKING INSTRUCTIONS

1. In a large bowl, mix crab, bread crumbs, eggs, mayonnaise, vegetables, and spices. Form 8 patties. Bake or cook them in oil in a cast iron skillet or other oven-frying pan for 4 minutes, until both sides are golden brown. If needed, serve with lemon.

2. Freezing option: freeze the frozen crab cakes in an appropriate container and separate the layers with wax paper. To reheat the crab cakes, place them on a tray in an oven preheated to 325 degrees F until ready.

SPAGHETTI MEATBALL SUPPER

Prep Time: 30 minutes.

Cook Time: 1-3/4 hours.

Servings: 10

INGREDIENTS

- ➢ 56 ounces of dried tomatoes sauce
- ➢ 2 teaspoons sugar
- ➢ 2 teaspoons dried basil
- ➢ 2 cloves garlic, chopped

- 1 teaspoon salt
- 1/2 teaspoon pepper

Meatballs:
- 3 cups soft crumbs
- 1/2 cup water
- 2 large eggs, slightly beaten
- 1/2 cup grated Parmesan cheese
- 2 tablespoons chopped fresh parsley
- 1 clove garlic, chopped
- 1 teaspoon salt
- 1/4 teaspoon pepper
- 1 pound ground beef
- 1 pound pork
- Hot pasta

COOKING INSTRUCTIONS

1. In a 6-quart soup pot, combine the first six ingredients and boil. Reduce heat, boil over low heat, cover for 1-1/2 hours, stirring occasionally.

2. For meatballs, preheat the oven to 400 degrees F. In a large bowl, mix bread crumbs with water. Let stand for 5 minutes. Add eggs, cheese, parsley, garlic, salt, and pepper. Add beef and pork. Mix gently but completely. Form into 1 inch balls.

3. Place the meatballs on a 15 x 10 x 1 inch greased baking pan. Bake for 15-20 minutes or until soft. Add the meatballs to the sauce and stir gently until combined. Serve with pasta.

4. Freezing option: Freeze the frozen meatball mixture in an appropriate container. Before using, it should be partially thawed in the refrigerator overnight. Heat in a covered pot, stir gently, and add a little water if necessary.

PUFF PASTRY CHICKEN BUNDLES

Prep Time: 30 minutes.

Bake: 20 minutes.

Servings: 8

INGREDIENTS
- 8 boneless half-skinned chicken breasts (about 6 ounces each)
- 1 teaspoon salt
- 1/2 teaspoon pepper
- 40 large spinach leaves

- 1 can (8 ounces) cream cheese
- 1/2 cup chopped walnuts
- 2 frozen instant pastries, thawed
- 1 large egg
- 1/2 teaspoon cold water

COOKING INSTRUCTIONS

1. Preheat the oven to 400 degrees F. Cut a longitudinal slit through half of each chicken breast so that the distance on the other side does not exceed 1/2 inch. Open and flatten the meat. Cover with plastic wrap and pound to 1/8 inch thickness with a meat hammer. Remove the plastic wrap. Sprinkle with salt and pepper.
2. Place five spinach leaves on each half of the chicken breast. Place 2 teaspoons of cream cheese into the middle of each half of the chicken breast. Sprinkle with a tablespoon of walnuts. Roll up the stuffed chicken.
3. Open the puff pastry. Cut into eight parts. Roll out to 7 inch squares. Place the chicken on half of each square; fold the other half of the pastry over the chicken. Press the edges with a fork. Combine eggs and cold water. Brush over the pastry.
4. Bake in a 15 x 10 x 1 inch greased tray until the thermometer reads 165 degrees F for 20-25 minutes.

TURKEY SAUSAGE-STUFFED ACORN SQUASH

Prep Time: 30 minutes.

Bake Time: 50 minutes.

Servings: 8

INGREDIENTS
- 4 medium-sized acorn squash (about 1-1/2 pounds each)
- 1 cup halved cherry tomatoes
- 1 pound of Italian sausage, remove casing
- 1/2 pound fresh mushroom slices
- 1 medium-sized apple, peeled and chopped

- 1 small onion, chopped
- 2 teaspoons fennel seeds
- 2 teaspoons cilantro seeds
- 1/2 teaspoon dried sage leaves
- 3 cups fresh spinach
- 1 tablespoon chopped thyme
- 1/4 teaspoon salt
- 1/8 teaspoon ground pepper
- 8 ounces chopped fresh mozzarella cheese
- 1 tablespoon red wine vinegar

COOKING INSTRUCTIONS

1. Preheat the oven to 400 degrees F. Cut the squash in half and remove the seeds. Use a sharp knife to cut a thin slice off the bottom of each half so that they sit upright. Place the squash in a shallow baking dish with the hollow side down. Add 1/4 inch of hot water and half of the tomato.
2. Meanwhile, in a large frying pan, cook the sausage, mushrooms, apples, onions, and dry spices for 8-10 minutes on medium heat or until the sausage is crumbled and cooked through. Add spinach, thyme, salt, and pepper. Cook for two minutes. Remove from heat.
3. Carefully remove the squash from the baking tray. Filter the cooking liquid and keep the tomatoes. Return the squash to the dish with the hollow side facing up.

4. Stir the cheese, vinegar, and tomatoes in the sausage mixture. Spoon into the hollow of each half of squash. Bake for 5-10 minutes or longer until heated, then use a fork to check the readiness of the squash.

CONCLUSION

I promised you healthy and tasty recipes that are easy to make and also fun for you and your loved ones, and I delivered. Nowadays, people are more and more aware of what they eat, and health is more important than ever. No one wants to suffer from diseases and other health problems. Healthy eating is an important thing you must always remember.

Indeed, choosing and switching to healthy recipes will be of great help to your overall well-being. A healthy lifestyle change can start with a few small steps. Here some simple reminders that will help keep your meals healthy:

- Make sure you get fresh ingredients for your recipes. When shopping, buy organic vegetables so that no pesticides or chemicals will affect your healthy recipes. If there are no organic vegetables and ingredients in your area, make sure to thoroughly wash the produce before using to remove any chemical residue.
- Reduce salt. This may be one of the most important tips for cooking healthy recipes—add substitutes instead. You will be surprised that there is no change in taste.
- Add fresh fruits and vegetables to your diet. These are foods that the human body needs and are important sources of nutrients.

- Avoid fat. Look for more foods high in fiber. Use olive oil or rapeseed oil low in uric acid, because they are healthier forms of oil. Also check the labels of processed foods. These are places where saturated fats can hide.
- Find alternatives. If you don't want to put meat in your cooking, substitutes include soy protein or TVP, also known as textured vegetable protein.
- Pay attention to the cooking process. In addition to the ingredients, cooking healthy recipes should involve healthy methods for cooking healthy foods including roasting, steaming, grilling, and stewing (although grilling food regularly may not be the best).
- Reduce processed foods. These are usually high in sodium content, which are responsible for high blood pressure and other problems.
- Use natural herbs and fat-free seasonings to help develop healthy recipes. Herbs can replace other processed spices and help you go natural.

Some recipes use different units of measurement. Here is a standard conversion table to help:

Common Weight Conversions
- 1 ounce = 28 g
- 12 ounces or 3/4 pound = 340 g
- 1/3 pound = 150 g
- 8 ounces or 1/2 pound = 230 g

- 1 pound or 16 ounces = 450 g
- 2/3 pound = 300 g
- 2 pounds = 900 g
- 4 ounces or 1/4 pound = 113 g

Common Metric Conversions

- 4 cups or 2 pints or 1 quart = 950 mL
- 1 teaspoon = 5 mL
- 1/2 cup or 4 fluid ounces = 120 mL
- 2/3 cup = 160 mL
- 1 fluid ounce or 1/8 cup = 30 mL
- 2 cups or 1 pint or 16 fluid ounces = 475 mL
- 1 cup or 8 fluid ounces or half a pint = 240 mL
- 1/4 cup or 2 fluid ounces = 60 mL
- 3/4 cup or 6 fluid ounces = 180 mL
- 1/3 cup = 80 mL
- 1 tablespoon or 1/2 fluid ounce = 15 mL
- 4 quarts or 1 gallon = 3.8 L

I hope you enjoy this book. I would like to invite those of you who have an instant pot in your kitchen to get the recipe book, *The Best 100 Recipes for Instant Pot Cookbook: Easy, Healthy and Delicious American Recipes for Beginners and Advanced Users* at https://www.amazon.com/dp/B084123D6Y. It has a lot of information that will also help you prepare simple and tasty recipes.

Made in the USA
Columbia, SC
05 February 2022